DO THE WEB WRITE

Writing for and Marketing Your Website

Christa,

Thanx for all your help. My back appreciates it. Your skill is considerable - you will have no choice but to succeed.

DO THE WEB WRITE

Writing for and Marketing Your Website

Dan Furman

Self-Counsel Press
(a division of)
International Self-Counsel Press Ltd.
Canada   USA

Self-Counsel Press acknowledges the financial support of the Government of Canada through the Book Publishing Industry Development Program (BPIDP) for our publishing activities.

Printed in Canada.

First edition: 2009

Library and Archives Canada Cataloguing in Publication

Furman, Dan, 1966-
    Do the web write / Dan Furman.
    ISBN 978-1-55180-832-1

    1. World Wide Web. 2. English language—Rhetoric—Data processing. 3. Web sites—Design.
I. Title.
TK5105.888.F867 2008   808'.066005   C2008-906240-X

This book is printed in Canada on 100% post consumer waste
Forest Stewardship Certified recycled paper, using plant-based inks.
The paper is processed chlorine free and manufactured using biogas energy.

Self-Counsel Press
(a division of)
International Self-Counsel Press Ltd.

1481 Charlotte Road
North Vancouver, BC V7J 1H1
Canada

1704 North State Street
Bellingham, WA 98225
USA

CONTENTS

SAMPLES

ACKNOWLEDGMENTS

Okay, I thanked all the usual people (mom, family, friends, etc.), in the last book, so we don't need to do that again (thanks for understanding, guys)! But even though I thanked my wife Maryellen last time, I have to do so again, because she really makes all this stuff possible. Her rock-solid demeanor, along with her loving (and understanding) persona allow me the professional freedom to do the things that I do best. I mean, it's not every wife who smiles when her husband holes himself up in his basement office for hours on end (and then calls him up for dinner). So thanks, sweets.

I also want to thank the folks at Self-Counsel Press (Richard Day, Aaron Morris, Selina Rajani, and especially my editor, Eileen Velthuis, whose deft touch made this book even better than it was). Truth be told, a writer is often voiceless without a publisher, and Self-Counsel has given me a voice.

In addition, my writing and marketing clients deserve a "thank you," because they make it clear to me that I do indeed "do the web write." Colleagues Jen Taylor and Guy Chapman deserve some thanks, as well. So thanks.

Lastly, and don't think I'm odd, but I'd like to thank my cat Gypsy for being a great office companion, and my dog Ruby for making certain that I get my exercise by insisting we take our daily walks. I'll get your dinner in a sec ...

Oh, and thank YOU for buying this book. I promise not to disappoint.

— Dan Furman

NOTICE TO READERS

INTRODUCTION

Too many websites do the web wrong. I'm here to help you do it right (write)!

Really — there are millions of websites out there that are just kind of sitting there, not helping their company in any way. Oh, they may look nice, but they don't do the one thing that you really need a website to do, which is to make a visitor take an action (buy something, contact you for your service, fill out a form, request more information, or similar).

In general terms, a website that doesn't generate action is completely useless. And most websites are just that — completely useless. This is because far and away, companies spend their resources (both money and time) on designing the website, and not enough on what information / content actually goes into it.

This book is here to change that.

Let's Start at the Beginning

Okay, so you have (or want) a website. Now what?

In all honesty, that's probably the hardest part of having a website; answering that "now what" question. Making a website isn't all that tough. If you know HTML, you can do the nuts and bolts yourself. And if you don't know HTML, you can just go online and one of perhaps 4 billion web designers (most with clever '80s names like Trevor or Dustin) will be happy to help you.

But they can only make the website — they can't answer the "now what?" question.

What Do I Mean by "Now What?"

Before I go any further, perhaps I should explain what I mean by "now what?" "Now what" encompasses three very general questions:

1. **What will your website say?** (Self explanatory.)

2. **Where will your website say it?** (What pages, page order, etc.?)

3. **How will your website say it?** (How will you write it?)

These three questions have nothing to do with the nuts and bolts of actually making your website, **but they mean everything in regards to its success.**

They are also the hardest questions for any business owner to answer. This is because generally, a website developer will seek to get these answers from YOU (and not the other way around, like many people hope). In fact, here's how the conversation usually goes:

Web Developer: "Okay, I can make you the site … so, what pages do you want, what order do you want them in, and what are you going to say on them?"

Business Owner: "Errrr … " (Translation: "I have no clue — I thought you were doing this part.")

What happens then is the web developer (who almost always isn't a web marketing person) will attempt to do this part by asking you a few questions about you, your business, and your life. They'll find out that you are a family-owned business, that you have a great reputation, that your customers love you, and that you have two cute kids, all of which will make it onto your site. They'll also attempt to figure out what your business does (having a business name like "Uncle John's Live Night Crawlers" helps a lot) and make a page for that too.

The end result will be a nice looking, somewhat boring website that pretty much tells people all about your business. Which is really, really bad. Know why?

It's bad because nobody cares about your business.

Really, they don't. Nobody came to your website to marvel at your company history, to read about your reputation, or to find out the good works your company has done. They don't even care about the Golden Turnip award you won last year (I know, I know … it's a big honor. Listen, if it means anything to you, I care, okay?)

This isn't to say this information doesn't have its place. *Of course* you need to mention things about your company — even the Turnip — on your website. The trick is in *how* you do it. How (and when) you do it means everything.

This is because your visitor is decidedly selfish; he or she came to your website with a problem, and your website needs to solve that problem, pronto. In other words, your website needs to engage your visitor, address the reason he or she came, and then drive him or her to action (buy, contact you, bookmark you, just get that mouse clicking). Anything less is failure. Make sense?

Remember this — the goal of almost all business websites is to get visitors to click in some fashion. That's it — that's the goal. Don't ever forget that.

And that's the crux of this book — to help you craft a successful website (whether you are actually making it or you hired a website designer). I'm going to help you decide WHAT to say, WHERE to say it, and then I'm going to show you HOW to write it.

Okay, Who Am I, and Why Should You Listen to Me?

As you probably surmised from the cover of this book, my name is Dan Furman. I am a professional business writer, business and marketing consultant, and business author (my last book is entitled *Start & Run a Real Home-Based Business,* also published by Self-Counsel Press, and is available anywhere you buy books). I generally work out of my home, writing sales and marketing copy for all kinds of companies ("copy" is another word for "writing," in case you didn't know). I'm also an expert on the Internet and websites, and what makes them work.

I do not make that claim lightly — I am good at this, and looking back, I have a lot of experience.

To begin, right now, I make my living online. I sell my service (writing) to businesses all over the world. I have clients on several continents, and I rely on my website for almost 100% of my business. And this isn't some "systems" business, or affiliate marketing or anything like that. I simply use my website to tell the world about my writing service. People go to it, read what I have to say, and contact me to write for them — it's really that simple (come see me at www.clear-writing.com to see exactly what I do, although you'll see plenty of my website in this book). In other words, because I know how to make a website work, a good percentage of the people who land there are compelled to contact me.

I've also been around a long time. I've been online since the early '90s, and I had my first website in 1995. In 1997, I had the number one tech support humor website on the Internet, getting close to 20,000 visits a week. I've sold products online, I currently sell my service online, and I help others do the same. I've seen the Internet explode into the mainstream, and I've watched thousands of websites both succeed and fail.

Trust me, I know the Internet well.

And, because of that, the biggest chunk of my revenue comes from companies of all sizes that need their website copy written, and need their websites tuned up in a marketing sense. **My style of writing just works very well for the web**, and I am extremely knowledgeable about how to simply make a website work. Essentially, you can say that I answer the three questions — I help companies figure out what to say, where to say it, and then how to say it.

In my time online (and like I said, I was on the Internet even before Al Gore claimed he invented it), I've studied what works, and what doesn't work in regards to websites. So trust me when I tell you that **what** you say to a customer on your site matters, **where** your information is presented matters, and **how** you write matters.

The principles I will be discussing in this book are rather simple; nothing too complex here. They are also easy to follow and implement, but the most important thing is, THEY WORK. For just about any website, too: small, large, or in-between. They work whether you are selling a product or a service; and they work whether your goal is to get someone to buy something, contact you, request more information, or all three. They also work whether you're a giant corporation, or a small mom-and-pop organization (or in the case of the Night Crawlers, probably just Pop).

I've spent years writing and consulting for website owners, and all of the websites I am involved with have one thing in common: they work, and they make money. In other words, I know what I am doing.

What This Book Is

In essence, this book is a culmination of my experiences with websites. In all the time that I've been writing / working with websites, I've come to realize a few things about them: what works, what doesn't, and how to go about making sure your website has the best shot at success.

This book is not scientific or technical — it is the opinions and observations of a real person who has **real success** on the Internet. In very simple terms, my website makes me money, without a million-dollar ad budget, without any "techno tricks" that nobody understands, and without any "piggyback sales" type stuff (such as affiliate marketing or the like). All I do is use my site to tell people about my writing and marketing business, and my phone rings (and my email inbox fills).

This book is for any company with a website, or any company that wants one. It doesn't matter what size your company is, and it doesn't matter how large your website (or planned website) is. The principles I discuss here will help almost every website out there become more successful; and it will result in more sales, more customers, more contacts, and more money.

I'm going to help your website in several key ways. I'm going to teach you what to say (what pages you should have), where to say it (the order of your pages and what to put on them), and, finally, I'm going to teach you how to write for your website.

Let's take a moment and go over these three things in a little more depth:

1. **What to say:** This part is actually trickier than it seems — yes, we all know you need a home page. But what then? Do you know how to break up your services and logically present them on your website? How about reasons to do business with you? Should you have a page listing them, or should the reasons be worked into the text on other pages? A case can be made for both. How about answering frequent questions; should you have a Frequently Asked Questions (FAQ) section? (Yes, you should, and we'll go over that later.) All of these aspects are part of the "what to say" question, and they are not easily answered. The prevailing thought most business owners have is to make their website an "online brochure." That really doesn't work well — you have to be a lot more targeted than that. Trust me, your visitors have a particular mindset when they come to your site, and there are certain things that they expect from your website. This book is going to show you what your visitors are looking for in terms of information, and how to make sure they get it.

2. **Where to say it:** You're proud of your company history. It's even a part of local lore, and, in the case of Trigger McNulty's Speedy Collections, it involves a tire iron that still hangs in the office (a reminder of a simpler, albeit more painful time). However, as fascinating as your story is, your online visitor probably isn't all that interested. Nor are they overly interested in your awards, your staff, your building, your latest news, etc.

    Now, here's the rub — these things DO all belong on your website, they just don't need to get in the way of the important stuff (what you do, how much it costs, and how people can contact you). Trust me, clicking is NOT very hard. Your customer, if they are so inclined, will find the story of Trigger McNulty and the tire iron on their own. What I'm saying is your page order is very, very important. People need to be able to get clear answers from your website. Hitting them with a tire iron story (rim shot!) before they even know if you can help them isn't going to get you business — it's going to drive people away. So this book will go over the order your pages should be in, in detail, and how your information should be presented.

3. **How to write it:** I get paid good money to write web copy for businesses of all sizes. The copy I write engages people, answers their questions logically, and drives them to take action. And in this book, I'm going to show you how to write effective web copy. Now, I'm not going to kid you — I'm not going

to turn you into me. To begin, my wife probably wouldn't like that much at all (and I also get the impression from certain people that one of me is more than enough). Second, writing is not something that can really be transferred from one person to another. You're not going to write exactly like me (or anyone else for that matter) no matter what I do.

However, that said, the basics of effective website writing CAN be taught to almost anyone. It's more a style and format than anything else — I can take almost anyone and turn him or her into a better website writer, using his or her current writing ability. I'll show you how to make your pages interesting and how to lead visitors to take an action. I'll show you the formatting tricks that really work, and I'll teach you to write so people feel comfortable with you. This might be worth thousands of dollars to you and your business.

How Important Is The Writing On Your Website?

Let me explain just how important website writing can be. There was once a guy I did some writing for. Before he contacted me, he had this flashy site selling an e-book. It had all kinds of moving graphics, popups, etc. Really snazzy. But he sold squat. I told him that for his particular product, besides needing better writing, all the stuff was getting in the way. He didn't believe me, so I offered to prove it to him (this is back when I had way more free time than I do now. I could afford to take these kinds of chances in hopes of making a name for myself). I made a simple site (white background, black text; about the limit of my web design skills). It took me five minutes (literally). Then I spent a day writing the text.

You know what I'm going to say now, right? Within a week, and with the same amount of traffic, my little nothing page outsold what his old site had sold in the previous two months. All the jazz and graphics and such were crushed by a simple white page with just writing.

Words are THAT important. Give me a blank page and 3,000 words, and I'll sell just about anything.

Please note: This is just an example — and I don't do freebie challenges anymore.

I've broken this book up into ten chapters (and an intermission), and then within each chapter, I break things up into smaller, bite-sized chunks using subheadings (this is how I write on the web, so it's fair that I write that way here). The first two chapters are the most basic, because I go over website conversion, targeted traffic, and the fundamentals of a successful website. These may seem simple at a glance (for example, in Chapter 2, I tell you your website needs to be easy to read. Well DUH!), but the truth is, if it were all so simple and basic, then every website would be perfect, and there'd be no need for me to write this book. Plus, the basics give you a foundation — I cannot talk about writing individual pages until I go over what people expect from your site in general. So if things sometimes seem a little "basic" in the beginning, that's by design.

I then go into the essentials of page order in Chapter 3, and in Chapter 4, I'll get into website writing in a broad-based sense (it's meant to be an overall treatise on the theory behind writing for the web, and will serve you well whether you have one page or 100. It's also the longest chapter in the book — by a lot).

I then get into chapters devoted to specific pages. Now, obviously, I cannot cover every single page your company might have, so I instead go into the general ones (Home, About Us, Products/Services, FAQ). Also included is a chapter devoted to Search Engine Optimization (SEO) stuff, a chapter devoted to alternate landing pages and microsites (a very effective tactic, by the way), and lastly, a bonus chapter full of extra tips.

The book can be read in any order, but you'll probably get the most out of it if you read it from the beginning to the end, as each chapter builds upon previous chapters. In fact, that's the way I wrote it — beginning to end. But that is by no means required. If you wish, you can be a rebel and read the end first if you want. It's not like anyone was murdered or anything and I reveal it on the last page (to be honest, writing and website stuff is pretty safe and decidedly "murder-free" these days. You could almost say it's a little dull).

Okay, so that's what to expect out of the book. Now let me tell you what the book isn't.

What This Book Isn't

This book is not overly technical. In other words, I'm not going to get into the painfully dull programming and computer jargon of making a website. I am going to assume one of two things: that you or someone on your staff can code the website, or you are hiring someone to do it. When I talk about subheadings and bullet points, I am not going to tell you how to make them. I am also not going to tell you how to use File Transfer Protocol (FTP), how to set up a blog, how to insert links, or any of that stuff. That's what web designers and web developers (often the same thing, if you ask me) are for.

Speaking of design, while I will comment once or twice on design in regards to user-friendliness, I will largely remain on the sidelines in matters of how your website looks. Listen, I can code a basic website, but the truth of the matter is I'm really not that good at it (as evidenced by the practice template I'm including on the CD). I know how good design affects a site, I just don't always know how to go about getting it.

I'm also not very artistic; for example, I can't draw to save my life. Even my stick figures are odd looking, with one leg shorter than the other, egg-shaped heads, and squat little bodies. I drew a lot of these stick figures in school while pretending to work, and I'd usually put them in war scenes, where the giant circles (tanks) and flying triangles (planes) would further destroy my stick people. Despite all the practice I got (most teachers hated me), I never got better. But you know, I could write an awesome story on the battle that just occurred, and I could organize everything in a logical, easy-to-follow fashion. So what I'm saying is that design isn't my thing, but content is, and that's what this book is all about: content.

About the Pictures

On that vein, I want to mention the pictures in this book. The pictures are generally screenshots of my own websites (when I want to make a point of something that I'm personally using), and of a simple web template that I made for this book. The simple web template is indeed simple (just a header, link bar, and a big white space). But that big white space allows me to show you great examples of subheadings, etc., without the design distracting you; after all, this is a book primarily about content writing and conversion, so when I show you something, I really want your attention on what I am showing you.

I also did things this way in regards to pictures because there are no copyright issues if I use my own photos. I have neither the time nor the patience to ask other website owners if I can use their website in this book (it always has to go through a meeting, 14 approvals, and then a contract / release form. I have trouble writing a check, so I have zero tolerance for that stuff. That's partially why I got married — so someone else could deal with all the paperwork).

I also practice what I preach. And there's no better way to show you that than by using real-life examples for most of my concepts.

A Note to Web Designers

I love you guys (and girls). I work with web designers all the time, and I am in awe of your skill; like I previously mentioned, I cannot even draw, never mind make a three-column website.

I want to profess my fandom up front, because several times in this book, I tell the reader that most web designers probably don't know much about the specifics of page order and such. Now, I know firsthand that there are a few of you out there who know about the stuff I'm writing about here, but for the most part, the majority of you do not really offer these kinds of services (just like *I* don't offer design services). I'm just being honest.

I also don't treat SEO (Search Engine Optimization) companies very well in this book. Again, no offense: If you are from an SEO company and are reading this, let me state that it's my opinion that you personally are probably one of the good ones, and not one of the sleazeball ones.

I also joke around a lot when I write, so I do not want anyone to get insulted in any way when/if I make a joke or such. My jokes really aren't all that good anyway.

A Few Disclaimers

The principles I discuss here will help any viable business website. **However, this does not mean that every website or business idea is viable.** I get asked almost every week to do work for some fringe idea. Most offers I turn down because they have no shot at making it; I don't care how much you market, a cat-washing service isn't going to fly (although the cat might). See my book *Start & Run a Real Home-Based Business* for more of my feelings on this.

Also, not every *type* of website will benefit from this book. I am writing this book for REAL business websites that want to take visitors and convert them into customers/clients/contacts (this is almost all business websites). In other words, I am *not* writing this book for a company that wants to offer nothing but online games as a promotion, or a company making a "fake" site for a movie tie-in (however, I will say that many of the techniques I discuss here will help even these types of sites … it's just that I am not writing the book with them in mind).

While I'm on that fact, I find that my advice benefits service and unique product websites the most. This accounts for most business websites out there. Most sell a service (accounting, consulting, software development, writing, web design, web hosting, marketing, PR, plumbing, auto repair, jewelry repair, and the like), or they sell a specific, unique product line (custom software, custom-crafted golf clubs, handmade jewelry, etc.) So if that's you and your company, this book is almost guaranteed to help you. And if you're one of the few that wants to compete with Amazon, this book will probably help you as well, but again, I am not writing with those types of sites in mind.

Another thing: I am going to assume that you have a sufficient budget and/or a plan to deliver traffic. There's no way around it. Your website will not work if nobody visits. You don't need a million bucks, but you *are* going to need some advertising to drive traffic, and that probably includes a decent amount of pay-per-click (PPC) ads. I do go over targeted traffic in Chapter 1, and then SEO later on, but it is in a more overall sense — this is a website conversion/website writing book, not a "here's exactly how you get traffic" book. So please, don't be shocked when I talk about banner advertisements, and then leave you to figure out the nuances of them yourself.

I also specialize in succinct writing, and getting to the point quickly (heck, my website isn't called Clear-Writing for nothing)! If something I am talking about sounds overly simple, well, that's because it probably is. I'm very good at taking a topic and going over the whole thing in a few paragraphs; this is good, because I won't bore you. I've seen 50-page e-books trying to explain what website conversion is — I can do it in maybe five pages. I'm looking to make my point, get you to understand it, and then move on.

Say It Again, Dan ...

Here's another disclaimer. I want to point out up front that sometimes, I have rather strong opinions on a lot of things, and I may seem to repeat them over and over. I have these opinions (and repeat them) because I know, from experience, that the things I discuss work. I practice them every single day. So I'm not looking to debate anyone on the merits of page order, writing, etc. If someone thinks they know a better way, hey, that's great, but I'm not interested in an email debate. Write your own book.

Expanding on that point, let me tell you that *everyone* likes to think they have an opinion regarding websites. If you ask 100 people about your site, you will get 100 different ideas about what you should do. Don't be swayed. Unless the person giving you advice knows enough about what makes a website succeed to write a book on it (ideally with an overly clever title like *Do the Web Write*), they likely know very little about what actually makes a website work. If you want others' opinions, use the "Furman 21" (my website questionnaire) in Chapter 2 and on the CD-ROM included with this book.

It also goes without saying that the preceding rings true for everyone else in your life. Your cousin (who drives a paving truck) probably doesn't really know anything about marketing a website. So take his advice with a grain of salt. On that note, I'd like to point out that driving a paving truck is a fine profession; I mean no disrespect. Be it far from me to make enemies with an army of guys who drive trucks filled with hot tar.

Okay, I'm done giving disclaimers, and you're probably ready to get into the details of what will make your website work. So let's go.

1

UNDERSTANDING WEBSITE CONVERSION AND TARGETED TRAFFIC

Website Conversion Basics

We have to begin this book at website conversion, because in a nutshell, that's the entire reason for this tome: to get your website to convert visitors into customers. Everything I am going to teach you is geared towards turning more of your website visitors into customers.

But what does "website conversion" really mean?

Although it sounds boring and technical, "website conversion" is simply a fancy name for comparing the number of people who visit your site with the number that take the action you want them to take (buy, contact you, etc.) It is a number (or, more accurately, a percentage) that acts as a measuring stick for how well your site is serving you in terms of business. It's pretty useful, too, so I encourage you to read on and learn about it.

Your website's "conversion rate" is reached by doing a little math — don't get scared — it's pretty simple. All you need to do to figure out your website conversion rate is divide the number of "actions taken" by the number of people who actually visited. If 100 people visit your site, and 2 take an action, the equation is 2 divided by 100, which is .02 (or, more simply, 2%).

So when someone says their website is converting at 2%, this generally means 2 out of 100 people take an action.

> Conversion rate = the number of actions divided by the number of visits.

Hits versus visits

To figure out your web conversion, I am assuming that you will be able to get your website statistics to know the number of visits you are getting (your web host or IT department can tell you how to get this information). However, be careful here — many people look at their stats in terms of hits. This is a useless stat trotted out by IT people responsible for web traffic because it's usually a big number. Well, it's big because "hits" typically measures how many items load on your page in one view. To give a very basic example, if your page has just simple HTML and also has 4 pictures, one visit will typically result in 5 hits (the page load, and 4 pictures loading). Other things affect hits too, so ignore the "hit" stat, and instead concentrate on "unique visitors" (or similar). It's a smaller number, and won't make you feel as good, but it's a truer measure of how many people come to your website because it is literally the number of unique IP addresses that have visited your site, so theoretically, unique individuals.

What is an "action"?

I mentioned a visitor taking an action — but what exactly is an action? Well, it's whatever you need your website to do. For example, on my main website, at this writing, I don't sell products. Thus, I measure "actions" by how many emails and phone calls I get inquiring about my service. To me, an email or a phone call is a successful action. If someone comes to my website and then contacts me because of it, well, that's the result I was looking for.

So if you have a service-type business (which could mean local plumber all the way up to an enterprise-level software developer), your "action," in terms of a conversion rate, is generally how many people contact you for your service (or for more information or pricing). And, obviously, if you have a site that is selling a product, your "action" will generally be a product order.

It's entirely possible to have two or more conversion rates on the same site as well (because, as I just pointed out, what defines an action is entirely up to you). For example, if you have a site that sells a product, and you get an email from "Mega-Store Conglomerated" asking about placing a giant order, isn't that a measure of how effective your website is? Of course it is. It's totally up to you. If you wish, you can track your conversion rate for sales, contacts, bookmarks, etc.

Now, I'm mentioning actions and conversions, but I don't want you to get too wrapped up in it. Knowing your conversion rate(s) is useful, and we'll discuss how useful it is in a moment, but it's also not an exact science. For example, all "actions" are not created equal. Take me for example: To me, an email from a wealthy, ready-to-spend corporation regarding web copy is MUCH different than an email from a broke college freshman offering me a six-pack of his roommate's home-brewed beer to write his term paper. (This has really happened. I refused, but I must say, the beer sounded really good.) Yet, in terms of defining an action, I count both the corporation and the freshman as the same (I just don't have the time to quantify the "good" actions from the "I'll buy you a beer" ones). So your conversion rate should really be regarded as a loose indicator of success, and not an exact one.

Establishing your conversion rate

I told you the formula and criterion for establishing a conversion. So, how long do you give before you settle into a "normal" conversion rate? There are two answers.

The first answer is one to three months — that's a fair measuring stick — that will allow for daily or weekly spikes in traffic and business to sort themselves out. I would go the full three if possible, but I have also found that business is pretty predictable on a month-to-month basis. I'm just saying three because if the "one month" that you measure is a big holiday month (like December), well, that could give you a skewed result.

The second answer is ... there is no answer, because it's infinite. You NEVER stop measuring conversion. For the most part, your conversion rate should hold steady (as it's not a measure of how many visitors, but rather how many take an action), but even this can vary. For example, a construction company will have seasonal surges. So will a tax preparation service. The conversion rate in the spring for both of these businesses will (likely) be higher than in the winter, as more website visitors are actually looking for the service right away, so a higher percentage might take action. Make sense?

Again, no hard or fast rules. Just establish a conversion rate, and then check it every so often.

So what is an acceptable website conversion rate?

I want to tell you something else about website conversion that is often misunderstood. In my opinion, there are no set-in-stone, acceptable website conversion numbers. So don't get too hung up on it. Conversion rates are more for your own use than to compare yourself to others, especially others in different industries.

A 2% conversion rate might be great for one site, while it's lousy for another. Because the Internet is so vast and varied, there is no acceptable norm (and don't let anyone tell you different). I say this because, for some reason, certain people seem to get hung up on what a "good" conversion rate is (usually 2%). That's BS to me.

I'm telling you to ignore what anyone else says is a "good conversion rate," because they are different for every situation. Here are some examples as to why they are different:

- ✏ It's MUCH easier to get someone to click to contact you for a service than it is to sell a product. Thus, websites that ask for a contact usually convert higher than those that ask visitors to buy something.

- ✏ That said, it's MUCH easier to sell a $5 product than it is to sell a $500 one. So sites that sell cheap products usually convert better than sites that sell expensive ones.

- ✏ Traffic matters too. For example, if you sell live bait, you will convert better by attracting 100 people who fish than you will by attracting 100 people who are looking for a gourmet restaurant (just a hunch, but I have a gut feeling those people won't be calling you). Also, your ad budget will dictate the amount of "good" traffic you attract. Usually, the higher the ad budget, the higher the quantity of "good" traffic, and (in most cases) the higher the conversion rate. More on traffic in a moment.

- ✏ Lastly, no two sites are 100% alike in terms of traffic and/or conversion. What is good for you may not be good for anyone else. Plus, all traffic is relative; Amazon.com likely gets more traffic than "Bud's Bait." It's what Amazon (and Bud) do with their traffic that makes the difference.

How to Use Conversion Rates

Okay, I just told you not to get too worried about acceptable conversion rates. However, it's still pretty important (and useful) that you understand the basics of conversion (and that you know your own conversion rate). That's because once you establish a conversion rate for yourself, it is VERY simple to measure how changes to your website affect your business. It's a really great tool.

For example, if you track your numbers and have a steady conversion rate of 5% for several months, and then change the wording on a few pages and your conversion rate jumps to 7% the next month, you know you did a good thing. And if it falls to 3%, you know to put back what you had (you DID save it, right)? ALWAYS save the "old stuff" from your website when you update. I've "broken" my site more times than I can count by putting up what I thought was better content, only to see my conversions take a dive ... it happens even to us web experts.

In addition, looking at your website in terms of conversion rates makes it very simple to envision large business increases. For example, if you get 1,000 visitors a day, and get ten actions, you are converting at 1% (and for many businesses, this is just fine). Now, say you make a few changes (like the changes you'll make after reading this book) and your conversion rate goes to 2%. You didn't just increase business by 1%. You DOUBLED it, my friend. This is because those 1,000 visits are now producing 20 actions instead of 10. That 1% conversion increase (which, for most websites, isn't all that hard to do) represents a HUGE change. Increasing your conversions by even a single percentage point could profoundly affect your business.

Conversion rates actually affect your business exponentially even if the numbers seem very small. For example, an initial 2% conversion rate raised to 3% may seem small on the outset, but it represents a 33% increase in business. That's right! In this case, 1% = 33%. And if the 2% is raised to 4%, it represents a 50% increase, which means 2% = 50%. And if we raise it 3%? Oh boy, that's where the real fun begins (yes, I sometimes have a strange concept of fun. I'm working on it).

Let me tell you a quick website conversion story

A client once came to me and wanted me to help him write a few Google AdWords (PPC) ads. He wanted to bring more traffic to his site and increase business (he sold financial products). A quick chat about his site revealed that he already had exceptional traffic; he was getting close to 1,000 visits a day from interested prospects (he advertised heavily on Google). He was getting perhaps 10 inquiries a day, meaning he was converting at 1%. His goal was to get 20 inquiries a day, so he figured that if he increased his advertising enough to bring in 2,000 interested prospects, he'd reach that goal.

I looked over his site and recognized right away that I could help him not by increasing advertising, but by increasing conversion. His site was not very well written, nor was it user friendly. So I told him, "Why not try and get more out of the traffic you already have?" We talked, and he agreed with my assessment. I wrote up a quick plan for what to do. The first step was to change the page order a little, and get the most important information clicked on first. The second was to change the copy. Under my direction, he had his web designer do the first part, and then I rewrote perhaps four pages of copy. Then he put up the new site and waited.

He didn't have to wait long. From the very first day, with the same amount of traffic he always had, he started getting 30-plus inquiries. This kept up consistently for weeks, and then months. All told, his new conversion rate jumped to 3.5%. I more than tripled his business.

But here's the really neat part. Had he upped his advertising spend to raise business, he'd be paying increased advertising fees month after month. But because I used the traffic he currently had, instead he had a ZERO increase in advertising costs.

Now, some of you may be saying, "That's great, Dan, but he had to pay YOU." And yes, this is true. But my total fee was less than what one month of increased advertising would have cost. So after the first month, that part becomes irrelevant. But it gets better: Based on how much he makes from a sale, I actually paid for myself in one week. After that, it was all pure gravy.

And here's one more "even neater" part: This new conversion rate (3.5%) will almost certainly hold true even if he DOES decide to eventually increase advertising (as he obviously was willing to do before I changed things). So he could feasibly be getting 3.5% on 2,000 visits if he so chooses. ANOTHER doubling of business.

Nice little story, huh? And trust me, things like this happen all the time.

Website Conversion Rates are a True Indicator of Success

One more thing on conversion rates.

Looking at (and measuring) your website in terms of conversion rates cuts through the clutter of everything and gives you the definitive measuring stick of your website's performance. This is because sometimes your website's performance might not be reflected in total revenue. Personally, my overall revenue numbers fluctuate depending on the size of the jobs I am currently doing — yet, initially they all come in on the same quote form, and count as one conversion. My revenue is also determined by how well I convert my prospect once they have contacted me. If I have an interested prospect, my website largely did its job (it delivered me the prospect, and now I have to take over). So it's not really fair for me to judge my website's performance on revenue (or whether I close the deal), is it? If I'm getting a nice flow of interested prospects, and my revenue is still bad, my problem almost certainly lies elsewhere (maybe in my demeanor or my pricing).

To give a slightly clearer example of the previous, imagine if you were unemployed, and had a nice résumé made. You sent it out, and it got you a few calls or interviews. But then you proceeded to show up to the interview in shorts and a "work sucks" t-shirt, and (surprisingly) did not get offered the job.

Is it your résumé's fault that you didn't get hired? Should you change your résumé? Or is the résumé doing its job (delivering contacts and interviews) and the real reason you remain unemployed lies elsewhere? The answer is pretty obvious (I hope)!

To wrap this part up, in very simple terms, knowing your website conversion rate is probably one of the best ways to get a handle on how your website is doing. It also gives you a clear picture on how changes affect your business.

Okay, let's move on to targeted traffic.

Targeted Traffic

The second part of Chapter 1 deals with targeted traffic. I mention this along with conversion because it is a "backbone" issue that (technically) has nothing to do with your website itself, but has everything to do with its success. Everything I will talk about after this point, from the fundamentals of a successful website to writing copy for the pages, will assume that you are bringing targeted traffic to your site.

What is targeted traffic, and why is it important?

Targeted traffic refers to website visitors that are interested in what you have to offer. In other words, they largely came to your website specifically looking for your service, product, info, etc. They aren't simply randomly web-surfing, they aren't just curious — they are looking for what you offer.

This isn't to say that you won't get random traffic. Your website will get all kinds of traffic. There will be surfers and browsers, people who landed on your site for whatever reason, etc. You won't be able to help that. But you want as much targeted traffic as you can get. And you have to work at getting targeted traffic — it won't just find you.

Targeted traffic generally comes to your website one of three ways — someone searched for your site online, someone saw an ad on a related website (or in an email message), or someone saw an offline marketing piece that drove them to the site.

Regardless of where/how the traffic originated, it shares a single concept: Someone said, "Hmm, looks interesting" (or something like that. Don't quote me) and went to your website.

Targeted traffic is extremely important, because it's the very essence of how the web works. Fundamentally speaking, the web is a lot closer to the Yellow Pages than it is to TV, for example. By and large, regardless of how they got your website address, people will go to your website because they feel the content will be of interest to them and/or their situation.

How do you get targeted traffic?

I'm not going to kid you. Targeted traffic will likely cost you a few bucks. There's almost no way around that. You usually have to pay for online advertising (on search engines, online banners, etc.), and offline (well, that's self explanatory: brochures with your web address, business cards, and the like). If you are not prepared to spend money getting traffic, you will have a very hard time succeeding online. This is reality.

I know, I know … everyone wants low-cost/no-cost "guerrilla-style" ways to get traffic. Well, they do exist, but I have to tell you, in my experience, they are very time consuming, and the results are almost always substandard at best (they can be nice additions to your paid efforts, though). In fact, it seems the only people who benefit from this type of marketing are those who sell the information on how to get free traffic (making it not-so-free anymore). Smart, successful web people are ready to spend a few bucks on advertising, so be a smart, successful website owner and do the same. You can experiment with other, cheaper ways of getting traffic later once you are making money.

Okay, here's how you generally get targeted traffic:

1. Pay-per-click advertising (PPC): When you use pay-per-click (PPC) advertising through Google, Yahoo! (formerly Overture), or similar, this is advertising where you bid on certain keywords (keywords that people would search for if searching for you), and you pay each time someone clicks on your ad (usually anywhere between ten cents and two bucks, depending on the popularity of your keywords). This may seem expensive, and it *can* get that way, but I have to tell you, I love PPC, and here's why: The people clicking on your ad searched for your specialty, read your ad, and were compelled to click and go to your website. By and large, that's seriously targeted traffic. These are people who are really interested in your service.

Now, there are entire books written on PPC advertising, so I'm not going to get into the technical "hows" here — you can figure out "how" by going to these websites (Yahoo!, Google, etc.), and reading about their advertising programs. But, for almost any web business, you are going to have to engage in some form of PPC.

And not only do you have to participate in PPC, you will have to have a sufficient budget (this is the reality of today's Internet). I can recall rewriting webpages for a guy that had a budget of $2 a day for his PPC ads … That $2 delivered three people, and this was the only advertising he did. Suffice it to say, that's simply not enough. It is close to impossible to run a serious business on a $60 per month ad budget (to give an example, currently for my little home-based business, I'm spending ten times that).

I'm sure someone out there will argue with me on this point and tell me that they get thousands of people for free, but I gotta tell you, I've seen countless good web businesses go belly-up because they were underfunded in an advertising sense.

So PPC, with a sufficient budget, is the first way to deliver targeted traffic. And I'll have a few tips later in the book about actually writing these ads (in Chapter 8, to be specific).

By the way, most search engines that sell PPC advertising have built-in fraud prevention, meaning your competition can't sit there in his or her underwear clicking on your ad all day. So don't worry about that. And in all honesty, people generally do not do this. Your competition is probably more likely to show up, in his or her underwear, at your place of business (which would make for an interesting morning, wouldn't you say)?

2. Your other advertising: This should go without saying, but your web address should be on every piece of advertising you use — brochures, business cards, letterhead, Yellow Pages, billboards, radio and TV commercials, and even those plastic bags you hand out at the trade show.

I have to mention this here because there are many companies that do not do this. I'll never understand why, because a website just enhances any other advertising you do — having a Yellow Pages ad with a web address allows you to tell a consumer SO MUCH MORE about your business. Also, anyone who goes to your website from other pieces of advertising is most likely pretty targeted traffic, wouldn't you agree?

This can be extended whether you utilize expensive advertising or not. It really doesn't matter if you have a TV commercial or you are just setting up a table at your local craft fair and handing out leaflets — if your web address is not on your advertising, you are missing out. In fact, in some cases, the smaller of my just-mentioned examples (the leaflets) will probably result in more targeted traffic percentage-wise (after all, this might be a stretch, but I'll bet almost all of the people who go to craft fairs are interested in … I don't know … crafts? Except that one husband who was dragged along unwillingly. He's not interested at all. In fact, he's planning his escape, and will hopefully be joining me on the golf course in a few hours).

Now, attaching your web address to any "big" advertising like a TV commercial might, of course, result in lots of browsers along with targeted traffic, but so what?

A Bit of Advice on Web Addresses

It's fine to have a website address that's your company name (in fact, if at all possible, you should). But did you know that you can buy as many web addresses as you want (very cheaply, only about ten to twenty bucks a year), and easily forward them all to the same place?

This means you can have a website address with your "impossible to remember or spell" company name, and also have a few "really simple, catchy names" forwarded to the same place. If you get creative, there are millions of great web addresses still available (and with the additions of other top level domains, like .biz, etc, many more are now available).

To give an example here, say you are a plumber who specializes in water heaters. You already have a website for your plumbing business: www.jpmcgilloughcuttyandsonsplumbingcompany.com. So why not spend the ten bucks and get www.weinstallwaterheaters.com forwarded to your site as well (or even better, to a page or website specifically about water heaters)? You can put this address on all advertising that pertains to water heaters (it's also easy to remember when said on the radio). There are a million addresses like this that are available.

My company name is Night Owl e-ventures. So my "official" web address is www.nightowleventures.com. But I really use www.clear-writing.com as my main address (they both go to the exact same place, but which one looks better on a business card? And is easier to remember)?

---

3. Banner ads and email: Banner ads are ads that you can place on other websites. Most popular websites now have some kind of advertising, and some of it can be quite effective. Especially if you advertise on a site that is in the same general area of interest as your business is in (for example, a bike accessories company advertising on a mountain biking forum). You can either search for "banner advertising" for companies that can help you (they can even make your ad), or, if you see websites that you would like to advertise on, look for an "advertise with us" or "your ad here" statement somewhere on the page and follow that link.

Another form of advertising is by email. You can buy email lists of people who are interested in just about anything. If you do that, you can send them an offer that links to your site. Again, search for companies that do this. However, I will caution you here: Many companies who do this get labeled as spammers, so you may want to refrain from blind email bursts. An offshoot (and very non-spammy) method of this is your own client email list; that's definitely targeted traffic. Just save the email addresses of all your clients, and send them an offer every now and again. Heck, it doesn't even have to be actual clients; you can have a simple "sign up to receive company updates" form on your website, and send the people who sign up a periodic offer. This is a very effective marketing tactic.

4. Online forums: I'm all over the Internet, and I've been posting to forums (essentially discussion groups) for years. There are forums for almost everything. And for each one, I have my website address in my signature.

It's a really simple way to get traffic, and it's almost always free (see, I'm mentioning some free ways to get targeted traffic as well).

I post to all manner of forums; I am a regular on several small business forums, and they have gotten me good traffic. I am also a regular on some hobby forums, and my website address is there, too. Now, I'll be the first to admit that I don't get a ton of business from Fantasy Football forums (I am a big fantasy football nut), but hey, who's to say that "MRNUTZ44" isn't really the CEO of a medium-sized company, and might need a writer at some point? There's no harm in posting your website address in your signature.

Join some forums — some related to your business, and some not — and put your web address in your signature. There is no downside, especially if you post helpful stuff. You'd be surprised at how many clients will look in business forums for experts. I got started in my home-based business because I was answering questions on an e-commerce programming site (I did e-commerce programming at my last "real" job), and a guy who needed an e-commerce programmer was reading it and said, "Hey, this guy Dan knows what he's talking about. He's answering all the questions!" One thing led to another, and soon I was happily e-commerce programming from my basement (which eventually turned into writing). So forums can really be a great thing.

One caveat to marketing on forums like I am suggesting: It is considered bad form to do anything more than have a signature on most forums. For example, the business forums I post to have a rule: no direct solicitation. People are adults, and they can clearly read my signature, so I don't need to answer posts with a "use my service" post. So just do what I did. Be a helpful, knowledgeable poster, and sooner or later, someone who needs your service will follow your link and become targeted traffic.

Here's the signature I use on the business forums I post to:

Dan Furman

Professional Copywriter, Business Author, and Marketing Consultant

www.clear-writing.com — My business writing website.

Also check out my new small business book: *Start & Run a Real Home-Based Business*

---

5. SEO (Search Engine Optimization): Natural search engine rankings deliver great targeted traffic. People search for certain words and/or terms, and the search engines try to deliver the most relevant sites. But it is VERY hard to get a high ranking.

This is important, so I devote a full chapter (Chapter 8) to SEO writing and search tactics, where I'll talk about things like press releases, blogs, articles, and writing your pay-per-click ads (and again, a lot of these tactics are free). The key thing to remember is natural search engine rankings in and of themselves are free, which is ... in a word ... awesome.

Wrapping up targeted traffic

The lesson to learn about targeted traffic is simple, isn't it? You get targeted traffic from where people already interested in your service will likely look or where they gather. It's pretty basic. There's no real big secret here. If someone in your town needs a plumber, they will likely type "(your town) plumber" into a search engine. If you have a pay-per-click ad that gets triggered by those keywords (or your site comes up high in the natural rankings), you stand a great chance of getting that person to your website. And then, because you have this book, your website will instantly greet them, offer a clear solution to their problem, and then convert a certain number of them to contact you.

Substitute your own industry/town/situation for the preceding. The result is the same: Deliver someone to your site that wants to be there, and you have a great chance of getting their business.

See, this web stuff isn't that hard, is it?

2
THE FUNDAMENTALS OF A SUCCESSFUL WEBSITE TODAY AND TOMORROW

There are a lot of really good websites out there. And there are even more that are flat-out awful. And I'm not talking about fringe "personal homepage poetry" websites either (we expect those to be bad). I'm talking about professional websites, made by professional website designers, for professional companies of all sizes.

By and large, these websites aren't awful in a design sense; truth be told, almost any competent web design firm can make a nice looking website. No, these websites are awful because they ignore a few simple fundamentals that all successful websites need to follow.

Now, I'm sure you are thinking, "But Dan, if these things you mention are fundamental, wouldn't companies and web designers follow them?" And you know, on the surface, that's a fair question.

But the truth of the matter is this: Very few people really understand how a website truly works. Not in a technical sense, mind you, but in a functionality, end-user sense. They don't ask themselves questions like, "Why is the visitor here, and what are they expecting?" I've worked with countless web design firms, and maybe once or twice was that point brought up by them.

And to be honest, it's probably not fair to expect them to know that. After all, does a car manufacturer teach you how to drive? Or does the company that builds the building for a new store then go about marketing it? Of course not. So maybe expecting a web design firm to understand how to market a site is somewhat unrealistic.

However, that brings up a small dilemma. When a company has a store built, they have all kinds of marketing data that shows how the store should be built for maximum sales. They'll tell the builder, "Okay, we want the main door here, we want the main showroom to be such and such a size, and we want the customer service desk here."

But this doesn't happen with websites. Nobody says to their web developer, "Do it THIS way, because that is what works." And that's because the company having the website built just doesn't know how it should be built for maximum conversion. And neither do most web design firms. There just isn't much data and such in regards to web marketing — it's still a very young industry — because the professionals in website conversion are few and far between. But at some point in the future, there will definitely be a clear-cut approach to successful websites (which hopefully this book will be a part of).

Okay, let's take a look at what makes a successful website, starting with the beginning.

The Early Days

Part of the reason so many websites are awful is due to the fact that the Internet is still pretty young, and many people still act like it's the "early days," when just being online was a huge triumph. For example, if you were, say, a florist with a website in 1999, chances were very good that you were the ONLY one in your area. So you could get web business by just being there. Heck, I can still recall how cool it was for me to do my Christmas shopping online in 1998. I mean, it was really something.

How silly does that seem now? Pretty silly, right? But in 1998, it was definitely a new thing. I bought some gifts from some pretty awful sites, simply because I had no other choice; if I wanted to buy a particular something online, I *had* to use what was there. In other words, like I just mentioned, just being online was enough to get my business.

The sad part is, many web design firms still, to this day, advertise their services by telling you how important it is to be online, but little else. I still see web design firms saying things such as, "Your website is like an online brochure."

To be honest, no, it's really not. A brochure is about the softest, most passive form of advertising there is. The Internet is proactive, not passive. Having a generic "online brochure" website isn't going to work very well for you on today's Internet.

Like my 1998 Christmas shopping spree points out, there was a very brief time when having a substandard website could still net you great business. It's like TV: If there are just a few channels, it really doesn't matter if your shows are terrible, because there's not much to compare them to (which, in my mind, explains *Gilligan's Island*).

Early websites got business because the medium was so new, and the early web surfer (me) was just astounded that they were even there. ("You mean I can look at porn AND buy personalized golf balls for Christmas? Cool!") It didn't matter if the site was awful, because it was THERE. I didn't question it (just like I didn't question why Mr. and Mrs. Howell brought trunks of money and a full wardrobe for a "three hour tour").

But that changed very fast. Pretty soon, *everyone* was online, and the playing field (and the rules of the game) quickly took shape. People rapidly came to use the web a certain way, and websites had to adjust (just like TV shows adjusted … wait, they didn't. *Gilligan's Island* gave way to *The Brady Bunch*, with their one bathroom and AstroTurf lawn. Okay, maybe TV isn't the best analogy. Let's get back to the web).

How the Web is Currently Used

I mentioned that the web evolved. Two things happened: Websites became easy for any company to have made, and search technology became very powerful and simple to use. All of a sudden, the Internet was flooded with websites, and search engines like Yahoo! and Google made finding what you wanted fast and easy. These two changes had a drastic effect on how people used the web. Suddenly, finding whatever you wanted became very simple, and you could find a LOT of it.

In my opinion, this changed everything in regards to how websites needed to be set up. In simple terms, for the first time, "just being there" wasn't enough.

Think about this: Many of your website's visitors will come there after a search for what your company does. This means that they have an expectation in mind when they get to your site. Your website needs to address that expectation clearly and efficiently. Just being there isn't enough; this is because, unlike 1998, your visitor has a TON of other options, and a very limited attention span. You either need to let him or her know that YOU are worthy of his or her business, or your visitor will move on (just like I switched from *The Brady Bunch* to more believable, sophisticated fare, like *Fantasy Island* and *Mork and Mindy*).

Okay Dan, So How Exactly Do You Let Visitors Know They Should Use You?

Well, the answer will be revealed a step at a time. I don't mean to sound cryptic, but it's impossible to understand, for example, how to write a home page without first understanding WHY your visitor is there (that's why writing your homepage is covered in Chapter 5. There are other things to go over first).

For instance, now you understand the difference between "then and now" in regards to the web. It didn't take very long (what, two or three pages?), but you can now clearly see why "just being there" worked in 1998, but won't work today. Congratulations — you are now light years ahead of most website owners and developers in this regard. Let's learn some more basic stuff to give you a solid base to build on.

Laying the Foundation of a Successful Website

I have discovered several principles that almost all successful business websites share. They really are simple, too, once you really think about it. The trick is to not let the technology of the web get in the way; it's very tempting to sometimes choose style over substance. But in the end, substance (and the delivery of such) will win out. Again, like I said in the introduction, what you say, where you say it, and how you say it are the important things. It's really that simple.

The principles I am discussing here will ring true for as long as the web is around. I don't care what kind of technology the future holds, if you want your website to succeed, it is going to have to do these things. It's just like TV commercials. Now that TV is mainstream and advertising standards have been developed, the fundamentals of a television commercial for products and services remains largely the same as it was 30 years ago. The delivery and technology have changed, and old commercials may seem quaint due to dialogue and period influences, but the basic premise of showing the product and (in many cases) how to get it remain the same.

Okay, here are the basic principles of a successful website.

A Successful Website Answers Six Basic Questions

The overall premise of a website is really pretty simple. In fact, one could say it's almost elementary. In a nutshell, a business website needs to answer a few (six) basic questions for the visitor. And those questions are the age-old "who / what / when / where / why / how" (although not necessarily in that order).

To be a little more specific, your website needs to answer:

- Who you are
- What you do (what your company does)
- Why someone should do business with you
- What locations you service
- How does someone go about using you
- When do people need to do it (the action you want) (Um, now!)

The order given here is generally the order in which you need to answer the questions (although there are no hard and fast rules here. I'll be talking in generalities throughout this book. I am counting on your common sense to take what I say and bend it to your situation).

These questions are also meant to be answered over the realm of your entire website (for example, you need to answer who you are on the homepage in a "you are here" sense. Then, later in the website, you can answer that question more specifically on an About Us page). As I go into specifics of each page in later chapters, you'll see me coming back to these six questions.

Let's look at these a little closer.

Who you are

Explaining who you are to your website visitor is twofold. To begin, your visitor should know right away where he or she landed. This can be as simple as your company name and logo up top, and perhaps a brief welcoming statement in the beginning of the copy ("Welcome to Scrape-it Steel Wool Skin Pads, where we solve your wart and pimple issues forever"). The goal here is to simply allow the visitor to be certain they are in the right place, which is actually very comforting in a subtle way. Listen, the Internet is a big place, and letting a visitor clearly know they landed in the right spot is important.

Second, at some point, your website should also answer the "who" question a little deeper for those that want to know. There should be an About Us page that tells the company story, its values, and how it does business. There can even be profiles of the employees, pictures of the buildings, etc.

What you do

Okay, here's where it starts getting sticky. Companies trip over the issue of clearly stating what they do all the time. It often begins on the homepage, where they engage in corporate-speak that essentially says nothing: "Welcome to Maximum Unlimited, where we offer proactive ROI solutions that effusively embrace the unique paradigms of your overarching branding scheme." (No, I don't know what that means either.)

Then, the website lacks direction; there isn't a clearly defined "services" area, or important questions are left unanswered. Now I realize that not every website can answer every single question someone may have, but a visitor should be able to easily find out what you do. For example, if you are an electrician, I should not have to guess as to whether or not you do electrical service upgrades. I should be able to find this information out easily (more on how to structure this later, but for now, let's just remember that your website needs to clearly state what you do).

Why someone should do business with you

Here's another pretty straightforward question that needs to be answered. This question is special in that it really needs to be answered throughout your entire website. Every page should have reasons to do business with you. Even your About Us can tout your years of experience as a positive. Or your "guarantee" can be a reason why someone should buy from you.

This question can also be answered directly (for example, my website has a page specifically titled Why Hire Us. Or, some people may have a Benefits page. It's really a matter of personal taste (and the type of business you are in). You need not have a direct page for this, but in an overall sense, your website needs to clearly answer why I should do business with you.

What locations you service

Nobody should have to guess where you service. Now, for many companies (like mine, for example), the answer is "everywhere." Well, then let's state that — let people know that no matter where they are, you can help them. Or, in the case of, say, a tradesperson, the areas serviced should be apparent.

A small offshoot to the "where" question is "how big?" For example, I let clients know on several pages that I take on any size job from a single letter asking the judge to go easy on Cousin Jethro (really, I've done this) to writing the copy for a large corporate website. Anyone reading my website will clearly understand that I do both.

How someone goes about using you

A visitor needs to clearly know how they can do business with you. There needs to be a clear path to buying your product, or there needs to be a simple way to get a quote, etc. And it needs to be all over the place. At any point, your website visitor should have a very easy path to purchase, get a quote, or contact you. Some companies have a "quote box" on the top of every page, others have a "get a quote" statement worked into the text, and some have both. Regardless of how you do it, your website needs to clearly show how to do business with you. The general rule is three clicks: Doing business with you should be no more than three clicks away. Not three pages — three clicks. That means one click to get to the contact page, one click to open the email link, and one click to send. I should be able to do this from anywhere on your site.

When?

This is really a silly question. Of course you want someone to do business with you RIGHT NOW. In fact, the very nature of the Internet is that it is a NOW medium.

However, let me state that many, many websites fail miserably at this. Simple statements like "get an instant quote today" make a HUGE difference.

Okay, so there we have the six questions. Together, they make up the basics of what almost every successful website needs to do.

A Successful Website is Simple to Use, and Does Not Frustrate Users

In addition to answering the six questions, a successful website is also one that is simple to use. Again, this is something that a lot of companies trip over. And many web design firms gladly help them trip.

I think the reason for this is that, in general terms, many web design firms are far more interested in how the site looks to the eye than they are in how it works in a conversion sense. And companies think this way, too — they sometimes think it's better to have the latest and greatest on their website in terms of technology. So they tell their design firm that they want the site to open with a flash movie, complete with new-age style music and images of generic, multicultural businesspeople overlaid with words like "dynamic solutions" and "customer focused," which appear on-screen in a disturbing, Orwellian-inspired subliminal fashion. This is good if you are recruiting for a cult — but this isn't so good in business.

Your website should load in a few seconds ("few" meaning "less than 2," not "20"), and it should present a visitor with clear options (and no, "click to skip intro movie" isn't one of them). Your visitor should start getting answers to several of the six questions right away.

Now I'm not saying that opening with a flash movie is always bad. For example, it's fine if you are marketing to teenagers or you are a site for a new movie. But trust me, Joe Homeowner is not impressed with music and graphics when looking at your plumbing site (Joe has other concerns, like the rising floodwaters). And companies looking for solutions to their accounting troubles usually don't need their options presented in stereo.

The reason I am so down on forced movies and music and such is they get in the way, and (in the case of movies) they make me have to guess what to do next. Listen (well, read) very carefully — I should never, not once, have to guess how your website works; I should not have to search to find out what you do; and I should be able to jump off and contact you at any point. I do not need 14 different things vying for my attention on the home page.

So what this means is your home page should load fast, it should tell me clearly where I am and what you do, and it should present me with clear, easy to understand navigation options.

Now this might seem a bit boring, but I want a link bar — top, left, right — wherever. Regardless of how you do it, I want a clearly defined way to navigate. And nothing fancy. I don't want rotating menus that dissolve when I click them; that's fine for an angst-y "scenes from my mind's eye" personal website for a Goth girl named Winona, but for a business site, it's just plain annoying.

To give you an idea of how annoying this is, think of a DVD. Aren't some of them astonishingly annoying to use? After some forced trailers and three warnings to not copy the movie (unless you want black helicopters landing on your front lawn), you click on "menu." The picture whirls and jumps a bit, and then you are presented with several options. You click on "scenes" so you can jump to the scene where the monster and the giant robot first meet (yes, I admit, in some ways, I never grew up). After clicking on "scenes," the picture whirls as sounds of machinery play. It seems like they can't just show me the scenes, they have to have this huge graphic of a "scene grabbing machine" that delivers the scenes to me. After whirring and circling a bit, the machine stops and presents me with four little circles. In these circles are images of the scenes on this particular screen. I can either choose one, or ask "grabby" (I often name these things) to get me another four.

Elapsed time: WAY too long.

But of course, I want to watch the movie, so I put up with it. Sure, I could put in another movie, but it won't have monsters and robots (actually, given my collection, there's a fair chance it does, but my point still remains).

But for your website, I am in no way bound to stay. In fact, there's SO MUCH STUFF online, I will leave in a split second. Make me the least bit frustrated, and I'm gone.

Let's go one step further on easy — I'll give you two quick "offline" examples that illustrates how people like things that are easy.

Example 1

Maryellen (my wife) really likes cheap jewelry (thankfully)! Show her a huge display of $20 silver earrings, and she's in heaven.

She also has a thing for unpleasant, crowded little stores that sell this stuff. She LOVES these types of places. I have a thing for avoiding these places like the plague, so on our last shopping trip, I wandered around and people watched while she perused the jewelry counter ... and I made an interesting observation.

This store's entrance had several doors; a row of "normal" doors that you had to open yourself, and one automatic door all the way to one side. Would you know that roughly eight out of ten people used the automatic door? Even people coming from the opposite side where the automatic door was would walk PAST the "normal" door and use the automatic door. And these weren't people with packages — they largely had two free hands with which to open the door. But a huge majority would actually rather walk further than to open the door themselves.

I find that interesting.

Example 2

Later that same day, I went to McDonald's to pick up dinner, as Maryellen didn't feel like cooking (yes, yes, I know ... but have you TRIED their Angus Burger? I love a great cheeseburger, and let me tell you, this one is sublime). Anyway, I never use the drive-thru at these places (in the immortal words of Joe Pesci in *Lethal Weapon 2*: "They @#$% you at the drive thru") so I parked my truck and went inside to get our food.

It was then I noticed something very odd — the drive thru had a line of about six cars. But the counter inside was completely empty. There was a little red car at position number six when I went inside (just one driver, no kids). I came out with our food five minutes later, and the little red car was now in position three, next in line to order. I went in and completed my entire transaction, got my food, and this guy, who was there well before I was, didn't even order yet.

So it would seem that given the choice, most people would rather wait two to three times longer at the drive-thru than just walk inside. I find that odd, for sure, but it says something about how most people like "easy."

Just remember this in regards to your website. If you make it hard, and hard can mean something as silly as a stupid flash intro page that plays music, you will lose a TON of business.

People like easy. Never forget that.

What You Are Up Against

I'd like to expand on that last statement, "People like easy," for a second. This may sound a bit silly, but it should make you think. When online, you are generally always five seconds away from WHAT-EVER YOU WANT.

This means anything — shopping, games, job hunting, "talk about kids" forums, house hunting, decorating discussion, sports scores, porn — it's all no more than five seconds away. And your competition — they are no more than five seconds away either.

So frustrating your visitor in ANY WAY is not recommended. In fact, given what I have just pointed out, you'd have to be really stupid to do that. So lose the forced movies.

A Successful Website is Easy to Read

Your website needs to be easy to read. There are three ways that "easy to read" can be interpreted, and they all matter.

Font size and style

To begin, I mean easy to read in a "THE WORDS ARE EASY TO SEE" sense. I really shouldn't have to mention this, but it seems that, for some reason, Corporate America seems to think we all love reading 8 point type. Well, they are wrong — we don't.

Seriously, so many corporate sites have this teeny, tiny little font that is almost impossible to read without squinting. I don't get it —maybe for some reason they think it's professional or something. Listen up, Corporate America — do you know why they put "the fine print" IN fine print? They do so because they KNOW nobody will actually READ it.

Think about this logically for second, okay? Companies bury "the bad stuff" in a tiny font because they don't want it read. "May cause festering boils" is never in 14 pt font, right? Of course not — it's in the teeniest font imaginable — that way it's hidden. So is it fair to say that putting your sales copy in that same size font is kind of stupid?

Also, besides size, font style matters too. There are really only four fonts that I recommend for online business purposes: Arial, Calibri, Georgia, and Verdana. These four are very easy on the eyes, and they are easy to read — no guesswork involved. For the main body text, any one of those in 10–12 point will suffice for your website.

Trust me on this. I have experimented extensively with fonts, and I keep returning to those four. Out of the four, I like Verdana the best, but I do mix in the others on occasion.

Formatting

How your writing is formatted will matter. The web is a very casual, "glance at it" medium. Your text needs to be understood at a glance, because people will scan your page before reading it. And the "scan" needs to tell a story. This means a lot of subheadings and bullet points (kind of like I'm doing in this book). And no long paragraphs (to illustrate this, let's go back to the fine print — they put "the fine print" in astonishingly long paragraphs because they know that all normal people will give up four sentences in. In fact, the only people who will read the fine print all the way through are lawyers. I rest my case).

I'll get more into the formatting of your writing as we move forward into the book (specifically, in Chapter 4). But for now, just realize that it matters.

The writing itself

About a third of this book is devoted to writing individual pages and such, so for now, I'll just mention this little tidbit that I often use: You are an adult. You do not HAVE to read anything you do not WANT to read.

Right? As an adult, you are pretty much free to choose what you want to read. If something is boring, you can just move along, correct? However, the same applies to your website visitors. They do not HAVE to read the writing on your website — they must WANT to.

What this means is, your writing has to be interesting; it has to engage the reader, and compel them to move forward. And I promise, when you're done with this book, you'll have a much better handle on how to do this.

Time out — The Rumors Are True — Size DOESN'T Matter

Let's take a time out for a second and talk about business size.

I've already mentioned this, but it is well worth repeating. The size of your company or website really doesn't matter when it comes to these principles I am discussing. I say this over and over because there's a misconception out there that things like "conversion" and clear language and such are more for small businesses and product sites, and not for corporate sites. That's just not true.

As I'm writing this very chapter, I am also working on a client site. The client is a consulting firm that handles accounting issues for HUGE companies. I mean, my client works with Global 2000 companies, and the work they do saves these huge companies millions of dollars. And my client is no slouch itself — the firm is well-paid for its services, and has plenty of employees, etc. And here I am, writing copy for a little 13-page site that is decidedly absent of buzz-wordy corporate-speak. The site talks to the CFOs of these huge companies, and does so in a very informal (yet still professional) manner; "here's who we are, here's what we do, and here's how we can help." This site will do very well for them.

In fact, this stuff is even more profound with bigger businesses, because of the numbers involved. I'll say it to you this way: If my writing results in my client getting just ONE MORE job per year than someone else's writing — just one more — I probably paid for myself 100 times over.

I don't care what size your business is, or how "professional" your audience is. This stuff matters.

Okay, so how do you know if your website is following these fundamentals?

I'll be the first to admit that it is not easy to know whether your website is following these fundamentals. That's because it really doesn't matter what you think about your website. You can think your website looks great and says everything you want it to say — it doesn't matter. The CEO of a company can love how the website came out, be wowed by the look and the technology, and personally approve the content … and it's all completely meaningless.

There's one person whose opinion really counts: your visitor. That's it (well, unless you hire a web conversion professional. If one of us goes over your site, you should probably listen to what we have to say, but even then, your collective visitors' opinions trump even ours).

Your visitor is the ultimate judge of whether your website has the right information, whether it's clearly presented, whether it's easy to read and use, and everything else I've been talking about. I don't care if the tech people or the web designer says something is simple to use, etc., if your visitor doesn't think so, well, then it's not.

A good example of this is an opening movie or music. When websites have these, the button/link to skip the movie or turn off the music is always tiny and somewhat hidden. Oh, it's there, but I have to look for it. Well, I (like most people) personally hate forced movies and music on a website, so if the "off" button is not prominent (and I mean seriously prominent), do you know what I do? I leave.

Now, I don't care if you or your web designer thinks the "off" button is prominent. You can look at your site all day and marvel at it, comfortable in the fact that there is indeed a teeny "off" button on the bottom right. If I (your visitor) can't find it, I'm gone (just do yourself a favor and don't have music). Fair warning, I'm probably going to say this three or four more times before you're done with this book.

Now, a small caveat. When I say your visitor's opinion matters, I mean two things. First and foremost, I mean the actions of your visitors. That's the biggest opinion in question. If 100 targeted people visit, and nobody goes past the home page, your site probably isn't very intuitive to use.

Second, I do mean actual opinions of others. You should seek out opinions in regards to the fundamentals I am discussing here.

Now, I know what some of you are thinking. You're thinking, "But Dan, didn't you say in the introduction NOT to listen to other's opinions regarding my website?"

Yes, I did indeed say that. That's because I do NOT want you to simply come out and ask just anyone things like "What do you think?" or "Is it easy to use?" You are not going to get useful opinions then. You are instead going to get opinions of people thinking about the design and how they would change it (which they probably know nothing about). You instead want to get opinions of people that think like customers.

So how do you do that? Simple — you give them the following questionnaire.

The "Furman 21" Website Questionnaire

This is a questionnaire I developed which will give you a clearer picture of how people view your website. It seeks to get information, without asking leading questions ("Is the design easy to use?") The reason for that is, depending on who you are, most people will not give you honest answers to leading questions. If you are the boss and approved the site's design, do you really think your underlings are going to tell you your approved design isn't easy to use? Trust me, they won't. Telling the boss that something he or she approved of isn't up to snuff is a very bad career move (I have a lot of experience in this, as witnessed by my many firings).

Your customers/suppliers probably won't be completely honest with you either; they want to do business with you, so offending the boss is hardly the best way to go about things.

So this 21-question questionnaire (which is cleverly named the "Furman 21") is designed so there is no obvious "right" or "wrong" answer to any question. It instead seeks to get small bits of information which will give you a clearer picture of your website (note: the form is printed here in the book, and is also on the CD. The reason it is printed here in the book is I feel this is a very important thing, and want you to have access to it even if you lose the CD).

To whom should you give the questionnaire?

You can give this questionnaire to anyone — it's designed to get general answers. Give it to family, friends, employees, suppliers, etc. Give it to as many people as possible (preferably 20 or more) so you can establish any existing patterns with the answers.

The questionnaire is also designed to put a reader at ease; the instructions are very non-threatening. It's best to include an SASE (self-addressed stamped envelope) with it. That way, people will feel their answers are more anonymous, further enhancing honesty.

Now, it's very possible that you are in a specialized industry, and some of the people you give this to have no clue as to your industry. For example, you may make Phase 3 Masher Pellets, and the people you give this to don't even know about Phase 2 Pellets (the misguided fools)! Or maybe you're an accounting marketing consultant, and the rest of your family is comprised of gravediggers (which makes for a fun reunion, I'm sure). Give them the questionnaire anyway. Because one of the points of this book is that your website needs to be clear and generally understandable by almost anyone (in a very basic sense). Your gravedigger cousins may not know the finer points of a balance sheet, but they should get a general idea from your website of what you do. (Don't be surprised if they say, "I didn't really get all

of it, but I got the sense that you could help an accountant bury the competition.")
Trust me, morbid as that may be, that's exactly what you are looking for.

Okay, on to the questionnaire.

So what do the answers mean?

The answers mean whatever you want them to mean.

I don't mean to sound cryptic or vague, but that's the truth. This isn't a pass or fail test (although some obvious stuff means "fail," like if most people can't contact you quickly or find your phone number, well, that's usually bad). Instead of a "score" the results are meant to give you a picture of what is standing out on your site, how easy it is to understand, how it solves basic issues, etc.

It will also tell you how easy your site is to use. If people didn't visit a lot of pages, it's probably because it wasn't very easy to get to them (however, if they only visited two pages out of ten, yet gave very detailed answers to everything, this could mean your content is REALLY good and it kept their attention so much that they didn't have time to visit other pages). If people generally guessed there are 10 pages to your site, and there are really 40, well, why is that? It may be that 10 are important, and the other 30 are support (which is fine, but knowing this information will make you put MORE of an emphasis on the 10).

The questionnaire will also tell you how people view your company, and how clear your message is. For example, if your company touts price/value as a main focus, you should clearly see that in the answers. If you do not, well, you have some work to do on your message. Or if you are a local plumber doing repairs for home-owners, and people are telling you that the look and feel of your website caters to large businesses, well, you may have chosen the wrong design.

Of course, a lot of blanks (or very little information) probably means your message is murky and not very interesting (it could also suggest a really dumb questionnaire answerer too, which is why I suggest giving this to a good number of people). And, obviously, some of these questions may not be relevant to you (for example, for MY website, it's important that my name is remembered. It may not be for other companies).

In reality, the best way to get a "pass/fail" score is to answer these yourself in an honest fashion, and then compare your answers to the people you give this to. That will give you a definite idea of how people are viewing your site, as opposed to how you WANT them to view it.

This wraps up the fundamentals of a successful website. Hopefully, you are fully armed with information, and are ready to get into the meat of your website.

THE "FURMAN 21" WEBSITE QUESTIONNAIRE

To the reader:

This questionnaire is designed to help companies better understand how people view their websites. You will go to a website, take a few notes, and then answer a few questions. There are no "right or wrong" answers, so **please do not look at the questions (which are in Step 2) until after you complete Step 1**.

Step 1

Go to this website:_____.

Spend a few minutes there and click around if you wish (you need not look at every page if you do not wish to. Simply go where you feel like going, and read what you feel like reading). Also, take a few notes on what pages you visited, what you think the company does, what they offer, how the website strikes you, write down some information on products, services, etc. (But remember, this is NOT a test and you do NOT have to seek out each page and take detailed notes. Just jot down whatever strikes your fancy.)

After a few minutes (say five), close your browser and answer the questions in Step 2. If you cannot answer a question from your notes, leave it blank (do NOT go back to the site to find the answer, as that will defeat the purpose of this exercise. A blank answer is just as valuable in terms of information).

Step 2

Answer the following questions from your notes. Again, blank answers are fine. Please do not go back to the site until told to.

How many pages are on the site? Guess if you must. _____

How many pages did you visit? Guess if you must. _____

What (generally) does the company do (or sell)?

_____

_____

_____

_____

What services (or products) do they offer?

_____

_____

_____

_____

Who would you say is their main customer?

_____
_____
_____
_____

What general problems do the company's products or services solve?

_____
_____
_____
_____

Does the website mention an area served (town, state, country, etc.)? What was it?

_____
_____
_____
_____

How long has the company been in business, and do you know anything about its history or values?

_____
_____
_____
_____

Did you feel reasons to do business with the company were clearly given?

_____
_____
_____
_____

If so, what were a few?

_____
_____
_____
_____

Were there a lot of different places to click on the pages (not just a link bar?)

_____
_____
_____
_____

Did you feel the site made it simple to figure out where to go for more information on any particular thing, or were you completely lost as to where to go next?

_____

_____

_____

_____

Are the products or services expensive? Or are they value-based?

_____

_____

_____

_____

In your opinion, going by the look and tone of the site, what size company (or what income level person) would be doing business with this site? Choose only one.

Homeowners / Individuals ☐
Small businesses ☐
Large businesses ☐
Other ☐

Did the website mention anyone's name? What was it?

_____

_____

_____

You are finished with Step 2. Again, blank and incomplete answers are fine.

Step 3

For Step 3, you will go back to the site. However, when you visit again, do NOT go back to answer any Step 2 questions, even if you left some blank.

Ok, go back to _____ now and tell us how long it took you to:

Find out how to contact us in any way (quote, email, etc.):
Under 2 seconds ☐   2-5 seconds ☐   Over 5 seconds / couldn't find ☐

Find a phone number:
Under 2 seconds ☐   2-5 seconds ☐   Over 5 seconds / couldn't find ☐

Find out where the company does business:
Under 2 seconds ☐   2-5 seconds ☐   Over 5 seconds / couldn't find ☐

Find out how to buy/get (specific main product / service sold by company)
Under 2 seconds ☐   2-5 seconds ☐   Over 5 seconds / couldn't find ☐

On the home page, how long before you see the word "you?"

Under 1 second (it's staring me in the face) ☐
1-3 seconds (it's close to the top) ☐
Over 3 seconds (I sort of had to look) ☐

How many clicks does it take to "buy" or "contact us for a quote" from the home page?

One click ☐
Two clicks ☐
More than two ☐

Thank you for your help. You are finished. Please return this to:

_____

_____

3
PAGE ORDER AND INFORMATION TO INCLUDE

The page order (and, as an extension, just what pages to have and what to put on them) is an important part of the overall presentation of your website. It doesn't seem that vital at a glance (after all, no matter what you do, not everyone will navigate your website in the same order), but it is. Essentially, almost everything out there has a logical order, and your website should be no different. A book has logical chapters; a movie has a beginning, a middle, and an end; a phone book is alphabetical; and so on.

Now, I'll admit, this is not the sexiest piece of marketing advice you'll ever see. I mean, worrying about page order is akin to worrying about rotating your tires — it's necessary, but something that you don't really see any great benefit from. In fact, since it is so dull, we've started to shy away from this somewhat necessary maintenance service. NOBODY rotates their tires anymore. You go to the Quickylube place to get your car's oil changed. What's your response when the mechanic comes in holding a piece of dirty plastic and says, "This is your Dyrillion Smog Filter, and it's dirty, meaning YOUR CHILDREN ARE BREATHING IN SMOG … oh, and you also need your tires rotated."

The common response is a hardened, guiltless "No, thank you. Just give me the $19.99 special." That's because we've learned about these places. That piece of plastic probably didn't even come from your car. It sits on a table in the mechanic's area, and the guys take turns bringing it in to show people. They call it different names because they KNOW that we know nothing about cars ("Sir, here's your Masonic Ramrod Plug, and boy, has it seen better days!"). However, no matter what they call it ("Crankless Sloshometer") they always also seem to say we need our tires rotated. I guess since we (sort of) understand that, it adds credibility.

The downside to this is the one honest shop where a real part is truly worn out. Our kids REALLY COULD be breathing in smog, and we'd say, "That's okay, just keep the old one."

But anyway, never mind the kids (they're fine … smog builds character). My point is, tire rotation is necessary but boring, so most people skip it. And that brings us back to page order, which I don't want you to skip (you were wondering where I was going with this, weren't you?)

Let's (literally) start with a word on navigation.

A Word on Navigation

Okay, I am going to assume your website will have a link bar, or some form of definitive navigation (I'm going to call it a link bar from now on). This can be a horizontal link bar on the top, a vertical link bar on the left, or a vertical link bar on the right (at least one of these three types of link bars are present on almost all websites, with the top and the left both each being extremely popular places in which to place link bars).

Resist any and all inclinations to deviate from these three. The reason they are so popular is that they work, and people expect you to have them. One thing that website visitors do not like is tricky navigation. And let me tell you, I've seen some real winners out there (this last line was written with a rather sarcastic undertone). Navigation "wheels"; loop-the-loop navigation circles; navigation where the page name is hidden until you mouse over it; and plenty of other cute things that made the boss say, "Wow, that's really cool" when seeing it the first time. Too bad he or she didn't have me there to say, "Wow, that's really dumb," because stuff like that gets in the way of a customer trying to find information.

Okay, so let's establish that you will have a link bar. Now let's talk about the type of website you will have, what information it should have, come up with some pages for you, and then put them in order on your link bar.

What Type of Website Will You Have?

Here's where we really start getting into the meat of this book. Until now, it's been a lot of preliminary (but necessary) information, but here is where I really start earning my money. The first thing we need to do is figure out what type of website you will have.

For the sake of simplicity, I am going to assume there are three general types of sites, which between them will cover about 95% of all business websites: service websites, product websites, and "informational" company websites.

Service websites

Service websites are websites in which the company offers a service. These services can range from plumbing to daycare to writing to web design to accounting to carpet cleaning to software development (and on and on). The services offered can be local or national (or even international), and the companies can range in size from 1 employee to 100,000, but the basic premise remains the same (the company performs a service).

So the general idea is for the service website to inform the reader of the company's services, ideally through addressing the problems the services solve, touting the company expertise, and spelling out the benefits of the company's services. And here's a key component of a service website — the goal is really not to sell anything in a classic sense — the goal is to get a contact. Oh, the service website will still sell the services, but it won't be looking to get an order right there online. The company salespeople (or owner, whoever handles these things) will do that part instead. The website generates a phone call, email, or quote request, and the company takes it from there.

Conclusion: The service website looks to explain the company services, gives reasons to do business with the company, and seeks to get a contact of some sort (email, phone call, or quote request).

Product websites

Product sites try to sell a product (or products). The overriding goal of the site is to make a sale. I am NOT including large "multi-product" retail sites here like Amazon or WalMart, etc. Yes, they can still benefit from the principles in this book, but what I'm talking about here is a company (any company) selling its OWN products online. Maybe it's someone selling golf clubs they craft at home, maybe it's a knife manufacturer selling its products online, and maybe it's someone selling a business opportunity or an educational course. But the goal of all these sites is the same: create desire for the product, and generate an order right then and there. Yes, they can still tout company benefits like service sites do, but they won't do it in quite the same way. Instead, everything will generally be geared towards getting an order.

Conclusion: Regardless of the product or business size, the sales site looks to create excitement and desire for a product, and then seeks to get an order.

"Informational" company websites

"Informational" company websites generally exist because the company wants an online presence, but the focus of the site is more informational than anything else. To give you an example, my sister and brother-in-law have a jewelry store. They have a website, and for the longest time, they didn't sell any jewelry on it. But since they have a retail store, there's really no need to contact them for a service either. So, their website was more informational in nature. In fact, it was there generally to satisfy shoppers (like me) that think if you don't have a website, you aren't a serious business. It's also there to give hours, directions, and to somewhat sell their services (for example, they do a lot of repair work, so someone local searching online for jewelry repair can find them).

This type of site is also handy for larger businesses, like the company I used to work for; they were the world's largest pocketknife manufacturer, but they sold their knives wholesale, and didn't offer products to the general public online. Their site existed merely to give company information, company history, etc.

Conclusion: Informational sites offer information, and also seek to offer a good impression of the business in general. They do not actively seek a contact or a purchase.

The preceding three types of websites will cover most people reading this book. Yes, there are other websites, like corporate sites that seemingly go on forever, and sites that sell both services and products, but for the most part, they are few and far between. There are also other types of specialty sites (like fake news sites geared toward the viral marketing of new movies, etc.), but those are another animal altogether, and not the focus of this book. There are also some "affiliate sites" out there where people try to sell other people's products for a commission. Generally, these are operated by people looking to get rich quick, and thus are also not the focus of this book. Forget about getting rich quick and start a real business, okay?

Now that you have decided which type of site you will have, let's move on.

Information (Pages) Needed for the Three Types of Websites, and the Page Order

While they share a lot of the same characteristics, the three types of websites will definitely place a different amount of importance on the information presented. Each will seek to address a visitor's concerns, but a sales site has to focus on the products first (advantages, features, benefits, etc.); while a service site will instead focus more on the company's expertise and what their services can do. The informational site does a little of both. They all need to spell out reasons to do business with them, but (for example) a service site needs to be much stronger in this regard in terms of words — for a sales site, the "company" might very well be an afterthought, while the product takes center stage.

To give an example of this last statement, I did some copywriting for a company that sold soil. Well, not just soil; it was soil imported from Israel. In other words, it was marketed as soil from the Holy Land. Since this company was the only company doing this, it really didn't matter if we touted the overall company. Nobody would come to the site and say, "Boy, I'd really like a bag of this soil, but I'm not sure about the company's history." Instead, they'd read the site (which was 95% about the product) and either want the soil or not. They really had no clue as to the company history, its headquarters, or its officers, nor did they need to know about any of those things; it just didn't matter.

Contrasting that, a service company might need to go extensively into the company operating philosophy. It might need bios of the principals, etc., (especially if their experience is part of the benefit of doing business with them). This is all part of what you are selling. In fact, many times, a company's experience and values will be the deciding factor in a decision on who to contact.

Okay, let's get to what each page generally needs to tell, and the order in which the information should be told. I say "generally" needs to tell because I have individual chapters on these pages too, where we'll get even deeper into it. And the "order in which the information should be told" refers from left to right on a horizontal bar, or top to bottom on a vertical bar. Although visitors have complete freedom to click anywhere on a website (and they often will) they still generally read left to right or top to bottom. And while people go all over the place, I have generally found out from experience that the first page "after" the home page usually gets clicked on the most, followed by the second page, and so on. So the order you present stuff definitely matters.

Now, you can deviate from this (and indeed, I experiment all the time, so by the time you read this, I may have changed something on my own site), but the following has shown itself to be profitable and functional.

Page order and page information for a service website

First page: Home

A service site needs a home page that welcomes guests and lets them know right away that the service/company can solve their main problem. It can also have a few other links for specific services and such, but the focus should be on addressing the reason someone came and how the service/company can help. A little company info won't hurt if it's pertinent (such as number of years in business, dropping the name of a huge client, etc.). And as far as navigation goes, I like ONE link bar. You can have some other links, but don't give me more than two distinct places to look and choose — that's just confusing.

Second page: Why Us (About Us)

For a service site, I usually like the second page to be a page touting why someone should use you. For almost any service, it's about your expertise, your values, your business acumen, and your credentials. This can take the form of an About Us page, and/or it can be a page entitled Why Use Us (or similar). I have personally done it both ways and like the Why route a little better (I also have an About Us deeper in the site). However, one thing you need to remember is that the main focus of the page is WHY to use you. Even if you are going to call the page About Us, do NOT lead it off with company history and bios of the founders. Instead, tout your values and experience. You can always have a section further down the page detailing your history.

Third page: Services

Third page is services. Because your site is a service site, you need to have the services close to the front, but not before the compelling reasons to use you. There's a reason I feel this way; when people come to your site (remember, we're talking targeted traffic), they are already vaguely aware of the services you offer. For example, say you are a septic company. As long as you confirm on the home page that you DO INDEED unclog septic systems, it's better, for the second page, to offer up reasons to use your company over "Johnny TP's Sucker-Uppers." (That's a great name for a septic service, don't you think?) Believe me, somebody up to their ankles in refuse will go right to your services or contact page, but most comparison shoppers will want compelling reasons to use you. So give the reasons first (the Why page), and the actual services second.

But what if you have more than one service?

You may have more than one service. I totally get that — I myself have several. In short, one services page isn't cutting it. So what do we do here?

Essentially, I like to handle this one of two ways. Your first services page can actually be a page of links, as seen in Sample 1.

Or, you (or your web designer) can utilize JavaScript (or some other web tech) to use the "flyout" method, where putting the mouse over the services page in the navigation bar makes a myriad of other pages "fly out," as evidenced in Sample 2.

Either way works. In fact, I recommend you use both; I certainly do. If you put your mouse on my Professional Writing Services link, you get the flyouts. But if you ignore the flyouts and instead click on Professional Writing Services, you get taken to the page in the first picture.

I am a big fan of the flyout or link method because it keeps your link bar neat, and makes navigation simple. Neat, simple navigation is important, because if someone can clearly see where to go, and what you have, it makes it much easier for them to find what they are looking for. So if you have ten different services (and you very well might), use one of the two methods I talk about here; either have your link bar services page go to a page of links, or use the flyout (or both, like I do). See Sample 2 for an example of a flyout menu.

By the way, if you notice the computer taskbar in Samples 1 and 2, you'll see I have Chapter 3 open in Word. I was actually writing this chapter as I took these screenshots. It's also after 11:00 p.m. Yeah, you could say I kind of care about this stuff.

SAMPLE 1
STATIC SERVICES PAGE

SAMPLE 2
SERVICES "FLYOUT" EXAMPLE

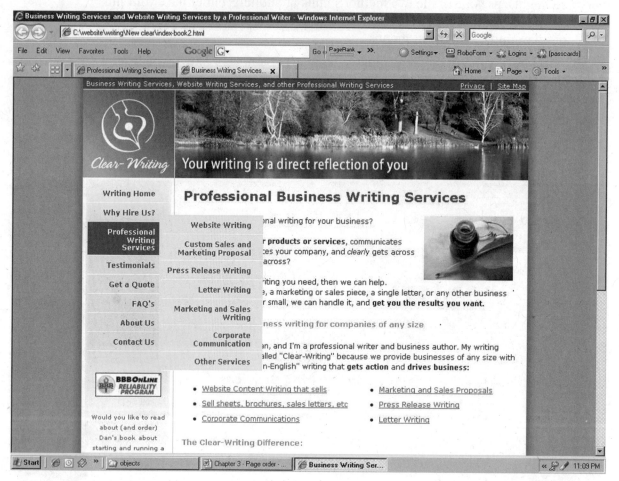

Fourth page: Testimonials

Next up is testimonials (as you can also tell from my screenshots, I'm following my own site here. I do indeed practice what I preach). I feel testimonials are VERY important for a service site, and deserve their own link. I realize that's a bit of a dilemma for a new business, but it's really a short-lived one. Once you do a job or two to a customer's satisfaction, ask for a testimonial. You're almost certain to get it. There's not much more to say about testimonials, because they aren't something you write, or should have written ... okay, let's talk about this some.

Fake Testimonials

There are fake testimonials all over the web. And I can spot them a mile away. There are two things a real testimonial needs to have: honest writing, and a real name / website link. You can get away with no website link on a few (one of my clients asked her name and website be withheld, but I put up her testimonial anyway, because I have nearly twenty others with links, so it's pretty obvious I'm not scamming here).

Do yourself a favor: If you don't have real testimonials, work on getting some. Do NOT write fake ones. They will hurt more than help. Having a testimonial like:

"'Great service. My feet feel great without all that inconvenient bloating.' Millie P., Straw Hat, Kansas" is SO obviously fake it literally screams "we made this up." Nobody talks in features / benefits speak like that. Trust me, you will get REAL testimonials soon enough, so if you don't have any yet, skip the testimonials page for now.

Fifth page: Quote page

Next up is the Quote page. I am a huge fan of the Quote page (I do recommend that you keep this page separate from the Contact Us page, but if you really feel the need, you can have your contact information on this page as well).

Simply put, your Quote page is a page that tells people how to ask you questions about your service. Since this page does not have a lot of writing on it, I do not have a specific chapter devoted to the Quote page. That said, there are a few key points that I would like to go over in regards to this page (please pay attention to this; I have found how you go about the Quote page is very important in how many contacts you get).

Key points of the quote page

- ✏ For most businesses, use the word "quote" in the link for it. I've done extensive testing on this, and so have some of my clients, and the proof is almost irrefutable; people LOVE the word "quote." It's a nice sounding word, it's a nice looking word … it's just a great word. I used to just use a Contact Us as my Quote page. Well, the minute I changed the name to Get a Quote, the amount of contacts I got skyrocketed. You can use different variations if you wish: Free Quote, Instant Quote, Get a Quote, etc.

- ✏ For some businesses, "estimate" and "assessment" are good words, too. If you are a tradesperson (plumber, carpenter, etc.), you may want to experiment with calling the page "Free Estimate". And for some larger, corporate-type businesses (where they do hundreds of thousands of dollars in software development), perhaps "Free Assessment" might be a good phrase. Bottom line: I encourage experimentation.

- Keep the Quote page very simple. Again, lots of testing went into this by me. The less I say on my Quote page, the better. I used to have an entire paragraph saying, "Each project is quoted individually; no job too small; sometimes small jobs are more expensive than large jobs, etc." It was stupid, and just got in the way. Now I just say, "Getting a writing quote is easy. Just fill out the form below, and Dan will get back to you within one business day." That's it. I do not know why I felt this great need to explain all kinds of things on my Quote page, but I did (many people feel this way). But I noticed a big difference in contacts once I lost all that garbage.

- Keep your prices off it too. Sometimes, I get four or five quote requests a day. And, as in any business, many of them are price shoppers who really can't afford me. During the normal course of my work, I do not mind this at all (I always end up converting a few). But, sometimes, that many gets annoying. So when I get busy and need to cut down on my quote emails, I put my prices on my Quote page. Stops things cold.

For example, I put general prices right on my Quote page before I started writing this book — I can't do my client work and also write a book while also answering five price shopping quote requests a day. I knew putting my prices up would kill new business for awhile, but I needed to.

Now, you may be thinking, "But Dan, if you put up your prices, all that does is keep the people who can't afford you anyway from emailing."

That sounds all well and good, but that is not the case — putting prices up on a service site keeps almost everyone from emailing. So if you have a service site, leave your prices off it (unless, of course, you want to cut down on contacts, like I sometimes do). If you feel the need to explain how you quote, do it in the FAQ, not the Quote page.

- Use a form. I find a form gets better response than a simple email link. I don't know why this is, but I'm not arguing with the results. Make sure you use some type of verification on your form (your web developer or IT person should know how to do this), because forms invite all kinds of spam.

- Lastly, use the Thank You page to your advantage. When people use any online form, it almost always goes to a Thank You page. Well, besides thanking them, use that page for something. Maybe offer a free downloadable report. Or give five additional reasons to do business with you. Or link somewhere (I have a picture of my book and link to my book website). But do something with this page — these people liked you enough to take an action. In other words, they are solid prospects. Give them MORE than browsers of your site get.

Sixth page: FAQ

I LOVE FAQs (Frequently Asked Questions), and so do web surfers. I often look at the FAQ to get my questions answered — it's a great way to explain the things you need explained, without cluttering up other pages.

For example, I feel the need to explain why I don't charge "by the word" or "by the page." I used to try to do this on my Quote page, but as mentioned previously, it just got in the way. However, the FAQ is the perfect place for something like this. An FAQ can be as big as you want, and contains all the information that you need to get across, but just gets in the way of getting a contact (like my pricing strategy).

Seventh and Eighth pages: About Us and Contact Us

If you didn't use About Us as your second page, put one after the FAQ. This page would have perhaps your company history, etc. I also like a separate Contact Us (meaning separate from your Quote page). To me, it kind of separates the two — people who want a quote go to the Quote page, and people looking to contact you go to the Contact page. And do me (and everyone else) a favor — put your phone number on your website. No phone number means it's obvious you are hiding for some reason.

Wrapping up the service site

There we have it: a nice eight-page site that will easily sell almost any service. It's clean, it's concise, it's logical, and it's very simple to find what you need.

Now, of course, you can add pages if you like (for example, sometimes I use a resources link on my link bar that has flyouts for writing samples, our work process, make a payment, free writing tips, etc.). I DO heartily recommend the flyout method for links, as it makes the link bar so much cleaner, and does not confuse anyone.

Now let's talk about a few other things before I move on to the sales site. There are a few pages that your site may need that I didn't mention — privacy policy, terms and conditions, sitemap, etc. I suggest you put those at the very top (like I do, as you can tell from the screenshot) or the very bottom of each page in fairly small links. They do NOT need to go into your main link bar — they just muck up your sales message with a lot of legal talk that nobody really cares about.

Now also, a lot of companies are trying to add pages to their site for SEO purposes (or have pages for company news, etc). I suggest putting links to these on the bottom of the page. (Sample 3 is the bottom of a new homepage I may end up trying.)

Oh, and I just mentioned a News page — if you can, stay away from this. Know why? Because: a) Nobody cares about your company news, and b) It's NEVER kept up. If I see a press release dated 2007, and it's 2009, you just shot yourself in the foot because you basically said, "We're too lazy to keep up our News page."

SAMPLE 3
PUTTING SERVICES ON THE BOTTOM OF A PAGE

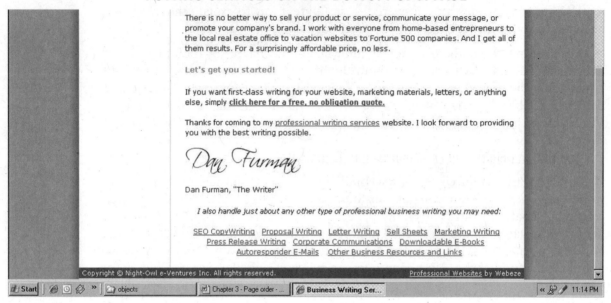

There is no better way to sell your product or service, communicate your message, or promote your company's brand. I work with everyone from home-based entrepreneurs to the local real estate office to vacation websites to Fortune 500 companies. And I get all of them results. For a surprisingly affordable price, no less.

Let's get you started!

If you want first-class writing for your website, marketing materials, letters, or anything else, simply **click here for a free, no obligation quote.**

Thanks for coming to my professional writing services website. I look forward to providing you with the best writing possible.

Dan Furman

Dan Furman, "The Writer"

I also handle just about any other type of professional business writing you may need:

SEO CopyWriting   Proposal Writing   Letter Writing   Sell Sheets   Marketing Writing
Press Release Writing   Corporate Communications   Downloadable E-Books
Autoresponder E-Mails   Other Business Resources and Links

Copyright © Night-Owl e-Ventures Inc. All rights reserved.   Professional Websites by Webeze

Okay, one last thing, and then we'll move on.

You can experiment all you want with this. I mention this because I am constantly trying new things, and looking to improve on my previous successes. I've become rather good at getting a website to work, but that doesn't mean that I can't get better. Most of the screenshots I'm showing you here are from my actual website, but by the time you get this book, it is likely that at least eight months will have passed and things could be very different indeed (in fact, the previous screenshot is my site opened in Arachnophilia 4.0, which, in my opinion, is the best web editor of all time. By the way, that's not my real signature, so don't get any funny ideas).

To give a quick example of this, Sample 4 is a screenshot of a new home page I will probably try out. I am stretching some of my own rules. For example, notice I am calling a page BOTH Quote and Contact. I'm curious to see how that works.

HOME PAGE

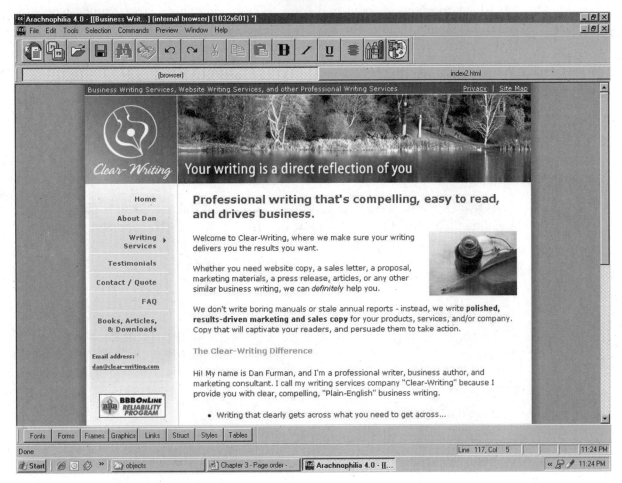

Okay, we're done with service sites for now. Let's get to the sales site.

Page order and page information for a sales website

A sales website is very different from a service website. A sales website has to explain more in fewer pages. That's because the more pages you have in a sales site, the further away from an order you are leading someone. As any salesperson will tell you: In sales you make your pitch, ask for the order, and then SHUT UP. If you say anything further, you aren't getting the sale. So a sales website needs to do the same thing. Make sense?

This is the main difference from service sites. A service website has a "soft" grey area in terms of getting an action. There's a "Well, it can't hurt to contact them" mentality sometimes, whereas a sales site is very black and white; either they buy, or they don't.

I have to mention again that I am NOT talking about large catalog-type sites here. For larger, catalog (or affiliate) sites, I don't have a lot of advice for you (to be honest, it's not a business model I am fond of). It's pretty hard to compete with Amazon and such. Also, I am not a fan of affiliate sites where the entire goal is to provide links to Amazon or whatnot. To me, these aren't adding any value for anyone (sorry about that, but as an Internet marketing guy, I am against these "make money while you sleep" things. It's just not that simple. Note that I did not say I'm against having an affiliate link or two. There are plenty of businesses that would do well to offer an affiliate type link to a product relevant to their audience. But if affiliate links are the entire point of your site, then we don't see eye-to-eye on online business. Sorry).

So when I talk about a sales site, I am instead talking about a company that is selling their own products on their site. Like perhaps a craftsperson selling their furniture; or a custom golf club maker selling golf clubs; or perhaps a software developer selling business applications. Or maybe even a coffee roaster selling coffee. These are the types of sales sites I am referring to.

First page: Home

The home page on a sales site needs to right away let the visitor know what products are available in a general sense. If you're selling coffee, the home page needs to say that. If you are selling golf clubs, tell your visitor that. And give them at least one CLEAR reason to buy from you:

"We have the freshest coffee — bar none."

"Our golf clubs will lower your score."

"Our investing software will show you returns far above the norm."

"Our body-heat activated gel will make her … "

Err, sorry. Anyway, you get the point.

Now, in terms of navigation, there are many different ways you can go. For example, for many types of items (like coffee, golf clubs, etc.) the products speak for themselves, and you're going to do a lot of your selling in the product descriptions. So, unlike a service site, a sales site can have many more links. I've seen many successful sales sites have a link bar on the top AND the side, with one of them essentially being a product menu (in all fairness, I've seen service sites do this too, but I don't recommend it). Remember, people likely come to a sales site for the products, so give them the products. If you have a lot of products, links on the side AND the top work fine.

In fact, if you have products, links everywhere can work just fine. I don't have a sales website myself, so I can't screenshot one for you. However, I'm sure my publisher won't mind if I use theirs in Sample 5. (I make these assumptions quite often, contributing to my many firings.)

SAMPLE 5

SALES SITE LINKS (MY PUBLISHER'S SITE)

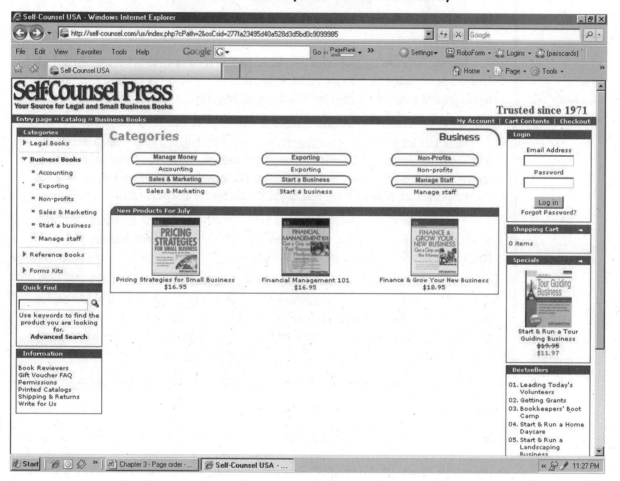

Look at all those links! They have links on the left, they have links on the top, and they have picture links, and they have more links under bestsellers … they have links everywhere. And for a sales site that offers a lot of products, this is just fine (in fact, it's ideal). They exist to sell books, not tell you all about the company history (you can find their history, but it's not front and center).

For many sales sites, I don't need to go beyond this. If you're selling a lot of products, offer up your products in a clear fashion — categories on the side, the products on each page, and tiny little links for the FAQ, About Us, etc. But there are other kinds of sales sites that need more pages (or are just one page).

The One-Page Site

Here under the home page heading, we have to discuss the one-page site too. This is useful when you sell ONE product.

Typically, these sites are hype-filled sales letters (usually running 4,000 to 6,000 words) that sell "business opportunities," but you can use this approach to sell anything. I've written a mini-sales letter (maybe 800 words) for a coffee roaster. And I myself have sold a specialized golf club via the sales letter. It can definitely be an effective way to sell a single product.

These sites are also handy when you just want to sell product, and don't want to be bothered with inquiries and such. The site sells the product, and that's it. There is no "contact us" or whatnot. However, like I said, this is handy for ONE product. If you have more than one product, the one-page sales letter site starts to lose effectiveness, as you have to bounce around too much.

If you don't know what I mean by the one-page sales letter site, search the Internet for "work at home opportunities" or similar — when you see a page with a screaming headline and lots of yellow highlights, that's a one-page sales letter site.

I'm not advocating hype, mind you (although there's nothing wrong with it if that's what works for you). A one-page site can just as easily quietly, and logically go over the benefits of your product and such, and ask for the order at the end (although I have to be honest, I recommend you buy a good book on writing sales letters if you want to go the one-page route. They are kind of special, and not easy to write. And no, I don't sell one, so take that as a completely unbiased statement).

Second page: Product(s)

Let's go right to the Product page (note, if you have a link bar for just products like I mentioned earlier, or have a lot of products like in Sample 5, just bump the following pages up one). After all, this is why people are at your site. They want your products, or they want to learn about them. Let's not keep them waiting then.

Since every product is sold a little differently, I do not have a chapter on writing about products (although I will go over it a little in Chapter 6). For example, if you have only a few products, you can perhaps devote a page for each right on your link bar. This gives you a clear path to them, and gives you lots of space to devote to them to create desire for the product. I wrote a sales site for a company that sold two different real estate software products: a profit calculator and a property manager. I wrote a short home page that welcomed people, and mentioned a few benefits the software offered. Then I devoted a 600 to 1,000 word page for each one. I went over the features and benefits, and had plenty of space for bullets, subheadings, etc. Then I did a short About Us page.

Their link bar looked something like this:

| Home | Real Estate Profit Calculator | Real Estate Property Manager | About Us |

The above makes for a nice, concise sales website that's selling two products. Very clear, very easy to navigate, and nothing to get in the way. This is how a successful sales site selling two products should look.

If you have a lot of products (more than you can put on a link bar, even using flyouts), then a page for each isn't really feasible (or even desirable. It's WAY too confusing, then). Instead, do what my publisher did and put the categories on one side, links across the top, etc.

Now, let's give a CARDINAL RULE on all sales / products pages: There should be a link to your shopping cart or order form on every product description. Do not make anyone guess as to how to order your product. You do NOT need an "order" link on your link bar. Have your order links right on the products themselves. "Add to cart," or similar, should be all over the place. You CAN have a "cart" link if you have a lot of products. But for two? There's no need.

Third page: FAQ

A Frequently Asked Questions (FAQ) section may not be necessary for a sales site. That's going to be up to you, because the selling is really done on the product pages, and like I already mentioned, I am not a fan of things getting in the way of selling product. So if you really think you need an FAQ, go for it (the rule generally is the more products you have, the more it's okay to have an FAQ, as there are already a ton of distractions).

But if you have just a few products, you can just answer any questions / objections right on the products page (in fact, that's a pretty elegant solution. I've written longish product pages that had a mini-FAQ built right in).

Fourth page: About Us / Contact Us

Make these one page if you can (call it About Us). It's much less in the way, then. And again, the theme is that if you have a lot of products, you may want to have more individual pages. Many sales sites don't even have an About Us page; they sell product, and that's it. And while YOU may not personally buy from a site that doesn't have an About Us page or a phone number, many people do.

Fifth page

There is no fifth page that I am going to recommend.

Wrapping up the sales website

Obviously, the sales site is very different from the service site. It's generally much smaller in terms of width (how many pages are on the main link bar), but probably a lot deeper in depth (as some may have lots of products/categories). The general rule to remember is the fewer products you have, the more they should take center stage, and the less you should say otherwise. The more products you have, the more you can say about yourself as a company (and look more like a conventional website).

You must also not have buying barricades or distractions. You need your products right near the beginning of the link bar, or if you have a lot of products, a second link bar with categories is a great way to do things. Make it very easy for someone to find your products, and then for someone to buy them.

There's not much more to say about the sales site. Except this:

But What About a Sales AND a Service Site?

Some sites function as both service and sales sites. A lot of software consulting/development companies fall under this category — they provide a service, and they also may have developed a software product that they sell.

For sites like this, I would generally suggest they be set up more as a service site (as almost all companies I have encountered who do this do MUCH more service business than they do sales). The product can either be included in the list of services, or given its own link on the link bar.

But of course, there's no rule that says a company can't have a service site AND then a small sales site too. (Read Chapter 9 for more on this.)

Page order and page information for an informational website

The last website we'll discuss is the informational website. If you noticed, my time spent on the sales website was shorter than the time spent on the service one. That's because the sales website sort of piggybacked off what I said about the service one. And the informational one is even shorter; in fact, I have no need to spell out a suggested page order, because it's generally the same as the service website.

In fact, the only real difference between them is the informational website pays a little more attention to the company and the About Us page, and doesn't offer so many convincing, hard reasons to contact them. Instead, they try to project an image (or "brand" in corporate-weenie speak). The Why page becomes a true About Us focusing on quality, longevity, company history, expertise, and other general "feel good about the company" tidbits. Also, a general informational site CAN have a news page (because your main goal is to give information about the company). Still, like I mentioned before, nobody really cares about your company news, but it fits better with the theme and goal of the site. Just, if you do decide to have a news page, please, please, PLEASE keep it updated and current. Otherwise, don't bother having one.

Whew … done with this chapter now. I tried to make this as interesting as I could, but in re-reading, I noticed this is easily the least fun chapter I have ever written (that even includes the lawyer and accounting chapters of my last book, *Start & Run a Real Home-Based Business*). Well, I did say up front that it wasn't a very sexy topic, but it is entirely necessary, and I hope you got a nugget or two out of it. Look at it this way: If all you learned in this chapter was to use the word "quote" on your service site, you probably just paid for this book 1,000 times over. And we still have seven more chapters to go!

4

DAN'S 11 RULES OF EFFECTIVE WEBSITE WRITING

Okay, it's time to discuss website writing. Or writing for the web. Or writing website copy …

Whichever name you prefer (and I'll generally be calling it web copy from here on out), it's probably THE most important part of your website. In my opinion, it's even more important than design. Of course, me being a writer, one would expect me to think that, but think about this: Some of the most successful websites out there are those long sales letter pages that have almost no design at all. Some are just blank white pages with tons of words. And many of them convert very nicely.

Think about that: almost no design at all.

Now I don't want web designers getting upset. I'm not advocating that design isn't needed (don't come to my house with torches or anything). For almost all business sites, design is entirely necessary. In fact, it's VERY necessary. Bad design will drive people away before they even start reading. Throw up green text on a yellow background with orange spots (heh — it was completely unintentional that I chose the words "throw up" for that description) and people will probably leave rather quickly (and the one guy who stays is a perpetually stoned 60-year-old hippie who isn't buying anything, but really likes your colors).

So yes, design matters; it pulls (the right) people in. But, I AM saying that when it comes to conversion, the words matter more.

Website copywriting is definitely the main part of my business, so I'm going to spend some time on this. This is a long chapter (easily the longest one in the book).

Thus, to make things simpler, I have broken the topic up into 11 rules. This makes things FAR more manageable, and easier to read.

Since I am doing it that way, some of the advice may be repeated in several sections, and some of it might even seem to contradict other parts (this is because writing web copy is NOT an exact science). What works for one type of website might not work quite as well for another, and the only way to find this out is to test. So (as usual), I am expecting you to take these rules and tweak them to your situation (and test the results). In addition, these rules are basic rules, and meant to generally be followed no matter what page (Home, About Us, etc.) or type of website for which you are writing.

Before we start, let's discuss persuasive writing and action words. They are misunderstood concepts, and I see them in *every* book about writing.

I don't have a rule that says, "Here's how you write persuasively." That's because, taken collectively, my 10 (well, 11) rules will result in persuasive writing all on their own. Believe me, I have never once sat down to write and said, "Okay, let me turn on the persuasion." Yes, I advertise my writing as persuasive, because that's naturally what it is. And it's naturally that way because of my rules. Follow my rules and you'll be persuasive.

I also do not believe that there is a mystical set of action words that will magically transform your writing. I know this isn't conventional thinking; every "marketing writing" book I have ever read says to use action words. Well, I'm not going to tell you to do that. Instead, I will give you some very effective "confidence" words and phrases in Rule 7. But these are to be used in addition to your writing, not in place of anything. I do not believe in forcing you to do anything in regards to writing. So instead, use these 11 rules that you fit into your current writing.

In other words, I'm not here to change your writing. I'm here to help make your writing (and your web copy) better. There's a big difference.

Rule 1: Web Copy Must be Scan-able

The most important rule of writing great web copy is that web copy must be scan-able. You can be an average writer and still write effective web copy if you follow this one rule.

What I mean by "scan-able" is a visitor should be able to glance at the page and know what it's generally about, and also understand the most salient points. This is important because people read websites differently than they read other things (like newspapers, books, or other print media). They don't read word for word from the start; instead they "scan" the page to see if it's something that they want to invest the effort in reading. And if something catches their eye, they'll start reading right then and there, and not at the beginning.

Notice that I also said "invest the effort." There's a reason for that.

See, we don't realize it, but reading on a computer is harder than reading a book, magazine, or newspaper. Computer eye strain is very real. In fact, I personally need glasses when working on the computer, but don't need them for anything else (the upside here is my wife thinks I look cute in them ... although I'm not sure I want to look cute). The thing is, we really don't realize the extra effort online reading takes while we are doing it, so it's generally unnoticeable. But the bottom line is it's harder to read online content, so without even realizing it, we scan webpages before we start reading them.

Now, we scan other places too. After all, we choose which newspaper stories to read based on the headline, right? But my point is we do this even MORE so online, so your web copy must be scan-able over the entire page. If it isn't, you will have a very hard time converting visitors the way you want to.

So how do you get your web copy to be scan-able? You'll use three things in general:

- ✏ Headlines
- ✏ Subheadings
- ✏ Bullet Points (like now)

Let's look closer at these three items.

Headlines

Headlines lead off most pages. They capture interest and/or give the reader an idea of what to expect on a page. You don't HAVE to have a headline, but I use them on most pages I write because it just helps lead things off. When people scan a page, they see the headline first.

Now, there are a lot of opinions regarding headlines. Generally the strongest opinions come from "long sales letter" copywriters and the like — these types of sales pages need a compelling, benefit-laden headline that typically asks a question or makes some kind of outrageous proclamation designed to spur certain feelings of need. In fact, there have been entire books written on the subtle subconscious effects of "sales letter" headlines, and how they draw people in to a page:

"SEE FOR YOURSELF HOW THIS LAZY SLUG OF A MAN WHO SMELLS LIKE MOTHBALLS MAKES $6,000 A DAY WHILE LYING IN SATIN SHEETS AND BEING SERVED ICE CREAM BY A SUPERMODEL! "

Okay, so maybe the subconscious effect isn't all that subtle.

Anyway, while hype is useful, and has its place, I personally prefer (and use) more fact-based headlines than hype-filled ones. And for most businesses, you will find this to be true and hopefully do the same.

Hype versus fact

I need to mention hype versus fact because every single book I have ever seen on headlines subscribes to the hype method. They talk about the subconscious effect I mentioned, they talk about "hypnotic writing," they talk about how "people want benefits, so give them benefits," etc. And they tell you how to persuade people by selling them stuff they don't need with a few strong words!

You know what I say? Give people what they are expecting. If they are expecting hype and benefits, give them hype and benefits. And if they are expecting solid information, give them solid information.

Like on my own website. Here's the screenshot of the new page I showed you in Chapter 3 (Sample 4) again.

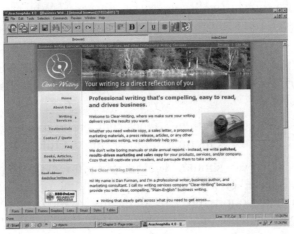

The headline here is "Professional writing that's compelling, easy to read, and drives business." I'm going to test this one later this summer.

Do you want to know why I'm testing that headline? It's because I feel that most people who come to my site are looking for (gasp) professional writing that's compelling, easy to read, and drives business (or something like that). Again, I'm of the opinion that your headline must address the main reason people came.

Now some fans of hype might disagree. They might say, "Yeah, but Dan, why not sell them what they REALLY want, which is higher sales?" I tend to disagree with that line of thinking for a site like mine. A headline of, "Let Dan increase your sales with his effective web copy" does not work well for my site (or many professional service-type sites). It MIGHT work well for a site that is specifically targeted to increasing web sales; if I had a small website where the theme was "higher sales for your website," yes, that might work. But my site is a professional writing site. I may at some point make a small offshoot site for increasing sales, and I might explore (and test) other headlines then.

Now I want to stay on this thought for a second longer, because the hype person (we'll call him Mr. Hype for short) might still want argue with me on this (good luck with that. It's MY book, so I'm definitely getting the last word). He might point out that the only reason one needs professional writing is to drive higher sales / more money, and my headline should address that.

And you know what? He's kinda/sorta got me on this one. Yes, that is what people really want. I have to admit that. People hire me to write because I'm profitable to them.

So here's my retort: Why stop there? Since we're psychoanalyzing my web visitors, let's dig deeper, shall we? What do we all REALLY want? Why do we get dressed? Why do we shower (well, some of us, anyway)? Why go to work? Why put up with idiot bosses? Let's address these wants in my new headline to make Mr. Hype happy.

"SLEEP LATE EVERY DAY, HAVE TONS OF GREAT SEX, MAKE MILLIONS WITHOUT WORKING, AND EAT ANYTHING YOU WANT WITHOUT GAINING AN OUNCE!"

There, have I covered everything? Does that pretty much address everyone's basic wants? Should I throw something about a car or a full head of hair in there?

My point here is that you shouldn't get too cute in regards to headlines. If your product or service is based on HOPE (like work at home opportunities, weight loss products, attract a mate potions, etc.), by all means, go the hype route. Immediately spell out the best case scenario benefit (make millions and get the girl too!) and take it from there.

As I already mentioned, for most businesses, I like headlines that generally give the reader information about the page they landed on. The headline lets them know they came to the right place, and encourages them to read further. And yes, they can be emotional without being hype filled. Here are a few examples of headlines I have written in the past.

For a Hawaiian "swim with the dolphins" tour:

"Swimming with the dolphins is an experience that you will remember — and cherish — for the rest of your life."

Now, the people coming to this site were expecting some kind of Hawaiian dolphin tour. They may not have been clear if they actually swam with dolphins, or just took a boat ride to see them, so they headline basically covers both — it's clearly about a dolphin tour, and yeah, you get to swim with them (that does sound fun, doesn't it?)

Here's another headline I wrote for a voice mail / VOIP company's home page:

"Dependable Voice Mail and VOIP Solutions for Your Company"

Nothing sexy or outrageous here, but if you were looking for voice mail (or VOIP), this would perfectly state that the information you want is right there. And that's what my clients were looking for.

Now this almost seems obvious, but it really isn't. Before I wrote the web copy for my voice mail client, the headline was more results-oriented (because that's probably what some web copy book said to do). It was something like "Never miss a call again." Well, that's all well and good, but it's really a pretty narrow focus. I realize voice mail exists so you don't miss calls, but is anyone really thinking "I don't want to miss calls" as they look for a voice mail provider? Or, do they just say, "I need voice mail"? I don't know for sure, because (thankfully) I'm not in everyone's head, but I don't think I'm making too big a leap when I say they are probably thinking more along the lines of "voice mail" than "missed calls." I think it's because our minds already made the connection for us; we already figured out missed calls equals voice mail, so we look for voice mail.

This is true for most things we look for; we already make connections. When we want water to go from one place in our house to another, we look for a plumber. Yes, we really want the water to go from here to there, and that's the true reason we're searching, but leading off the website with "water moved through your house" is probably nowhere near as effective as "local plumber ready to help you."

Again, my point with these somewhat outrageous examples is that I don't want you to over-think these things. There's a tendency for people to want to get witty and clever when writing headlines. There's nothing witty or clever about the voice mail headline (or the entire site I wrote, for that matter), but it pulls business (which is exactly what my client wanted).

Okay, here's a headline that's (a little) more hype-filled:

"Financial Sales Professionals: Would You Like To Close More Sales, Achieve Greater Production, and Enjoy Lifelong Success?"

Not overly hype-y, but not super quiet either. This was for a very tightly targeted site that sold advice and coaching services to financial salespeople. It definitely speaks more of benefits than a simple "sales coaching here," but that's because the focus of the site was so very tight. And it was also somewhat of a hope-based site. Any type of coaching or such is like that. You almost can't sell any type of coaching without touting the results.

In fact, hope-based products or services are almost a reverse effect from the previous, in fact — our brains made the connection "coaching equals more success," so we expect to see "more success" as the leadoff of the website. A lot of sports coaching is sold this way: "be a better hitter," "tackle better," "break the other guy's arm in four different places," etc.

I hope the preceding gives you a good idea of headlines and how to use them. Write them, and then TEST them. And if you're not sure what type of headline to use (hype versus fact), test them both.

Let's move on to subheadings.

Subheadings

What is a subheading?

Well, you just read one. The start to this section (the single word in bold) is a subheading. It tells you (generally) what to expect from the text that follows it.

For a website, a subheading is generally a headline for a paragraph or a section of a page. Its purpose in regards to scan-ability is fairly obvious: if you scan the page past the headline, the subheadings jump out at you. So it makes it very easy to scan a page and get an idea of what the entire page is about, and what information someone could expect.

I'm going to be honest. I think subheadings are more important than headlines. I could have a lousy headline and great subheadings, and the page will still get read (or at least scanned). That's because, regardless of the headline, people tend to scan anyway. However, in the interest of "top to bottom" neatness, I talked about headlines first. But do yourself a favor, pay more attention to your subheadings. And use them on just about EVERY webpage you have (okay, maybe Contact Us or Quote pages don't need them, but most other pages do).

The two types of subheadings

In my opinion, there are two types of subheadings. The first is very simple to go over. It's called (by me) the informational subheading, and that's because it gives information on what follows.

Take a quick look at Sample 6 for an example (and here's the template I mentioned earlier, too).

SAMPLE 6
SUBHEADINGS

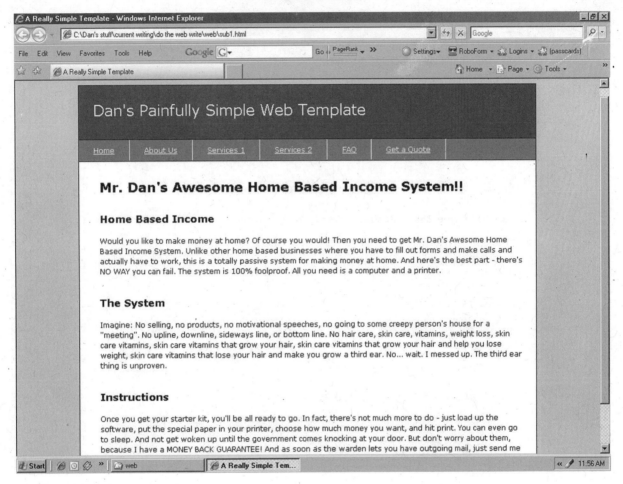

The Home Based Income subheading lets you know about what that paragraph talks about. The System one talks about the … wait for it … the SYSTEM. And the Instructions one lets you know instructions follow.

Okay, these are pathetically boring, bad subheadings. Unlike my general opinion on headlines, I like almost all of my subheadings to be a little jazzy. I almost NEVER use what I am calling the informational subheading. Oh, it does have its uses from time to time (i.e., the subheading Company History before the company history), but I'd say 80% of the time, I like to use what I call the Story Subheading. A story subheading (my term for it) generally tells more of a story. It's probably easier to just show you what I mean.

SAMPLE 7
STORY SUBHEADINGS EXAMPLE

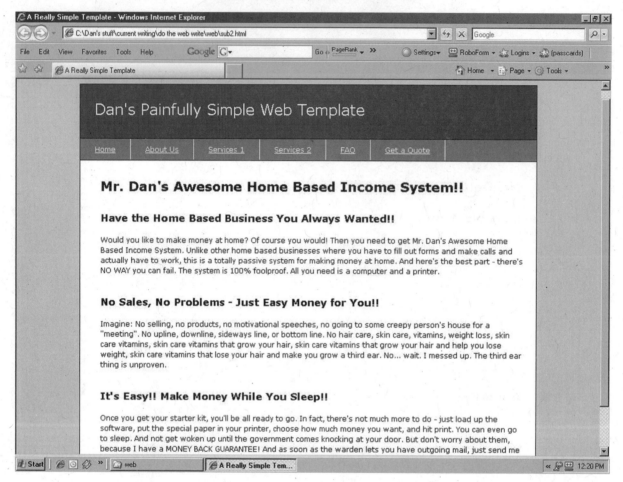

Here's an example of the Story Subheading, using the exact same page I did previously. The only thing I changed are the subheadings. You tell me which one reads better at a glance (see Sample 7).

See that? Isn't the second page MUCH better at telling a story at a glance? That's the whole point.

Now, I don't always use multiple exclamation points on my story subheadings, but I think you get the picture. The subheadings I am using for this page definitely "tell and sell" the product much better than the first, and they also make you want to read the page more (note to the government: I am KIDDING in the copy).

Here's another one from my actual website in Sample 8.

MORE SUBHEADINGS: DAN'S HOME PAGE

I have two subheadings here: "Crisp, succinct business writing for companies of any size," and "The Clear-Writing Difference." These are less hype-filled than my template samples, but they are also decidedly more "story" in nature than just boring old "here's what's next."

Generally, the thought behind the "story subheading" is to use it to somewhat advertise your company or services. In other words, the first subheading in the preceding picture essentially tells you that I have crisp, succinct writing (and, let's face it, who wouldn't want that?) So it announces what's next (well, sort of — it tells them my writing services are next), but it really drives home several points for me. The second one says that Clear-Writing is different, and also announces that I'm now going to tell you those differences.

Plus (and I'm going to break a small rule and get a teeny bit technical here), the subheadings are H2 HTML elements. So using the term "business writing" in the first one helps me with SEO (all of my subheadings are H2s. If you don't know what an H2 is, just tell your web person to make your subheadings H2s, and try to get some keyphrases in some of them).

How many subheadings to use on a page?

Use as many subheadings on a page as it takes.

Okay, that's not a great answer, but it's pretty accurate. There is no set number. In writing hundreds of effective webpages, though, I would say two to three for most pages is ideal. But if the page is really long, you might have six or seven.

The general rule of the thumb that I use is this: You should have at least a paragraph or two under each subheading. Sometimes three paragraphs if they are short, but I try to break things up into bite-sized chunks. A webpage is just easier to read that way.

Story Subheadings instead of Informational Subheadings

I mentioned a little earlier that informational subheadings have their place. But even in those places, I try to swap them out for story subheadings if at all possible.

Let me give you an example of what I mean:

"Company History "can become "Serving Anytown's Plumbing Needs for Over 50 years"(insert your own trade).

Then you have a paragraph detailing the company history. This also sneaks in the keyphrase "Anytown plumbing."

"Services Offered" can become "Marketing Solutions "(again, substitute your own specialty … I don't have to keep saying that, do I)? Then you list your services.

"Driving Directions" can become "Directions to our Anytown Bathroom Fixture Showroom."

In all but the most extreme cases, I will always try to use the story subheading. In fact, almost the only time I don't is if the web copy is for a fairly conservative, organization/website. Then perhaps the informational approach is best. And even in those cases, it's against my better judgment.

Okay, the last part of Rule 1 (yup, we're still in Rule 1 of effective website writing): bullet points.

Bullet points

Not much to explain here, as bullet points are pretty self-explanatory in and of themselves. I use bullet points a lot. Unlike subheadings, I don't recommend bullets on every single page, but I NEVER make a website without bullets on a few pages.

Bullet points allow you to make specific points in a very clear fashion. They also make for great scan-ability and are very simple for people to read. See Sample 9.

As you can see from my page, the bullets list the benefits of my website writing in a rather clear fashion (well, technically, they are features. It just sounds better to call them benefits). It gives readers a very simple-to-glance-at picture of my most important points.

This is an example of side by side bullets; two across and three down in this case (with a subheading leading it off). But I don't always do this. If there are only three to five points, I usually use one row, like below (and these bullets will list a few points about them):

- **Spacing is important:** Keep a space between each point. Bullet points lose their "ease of reading" effect when they are crammed together.

  And when I say "bullet point," the bullet itself can be anything; squares, diamonds, numbers, etc.

- **Important Note:** I also use bullets in paragraph form. There's no rule that says a bullet list needs to be an actual item list. This bullet is a four-sentence paragraph, and that's just fine. I often bold the first part of it to make it stand out.

- **Important Note Continued:** Look at Sample 9. These paragraph bullets are actually quite effective at conveying a point and making the text stand out from the rest of the page. The eyes are drawn to a bullet, and the "short-ness" of the information says "easy to read," and as we've already gone over, we LIKE easy!

- **Bullets can be links.** It's a great way to list services and the like.

- **Lastly, don't overstay your welcome.** Unlike subheadings, which I use early and often, I do not overdo it with bullet points. I use them on maybe 60% of the pages I write (not 99%, like I do with subheadings). That's because I feel the more pages you use bullets on (and the more times you use them on a single page), the less effective they become. If it seems like everywhere you look on your site you see bullet points, that means you probably have too many.

Okay, all done with Rule 1. The rest of the rules are probably not going to be this long.

BULLET POINTS

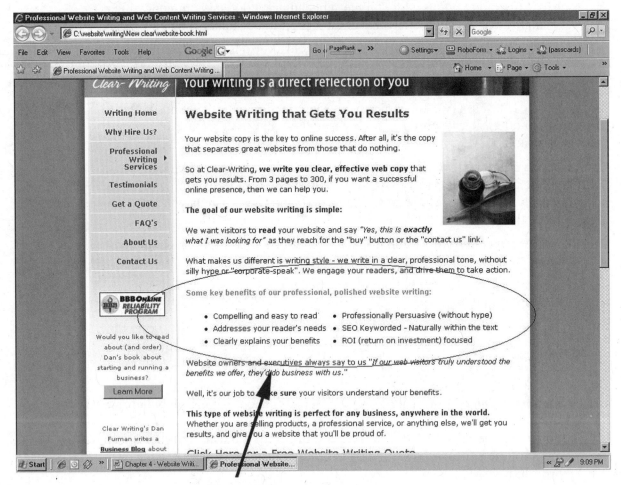

Rule 2: Use Short Paragraphs

I've already alluded to this rule about using short paragraphs somewhat in Chapter 3, but here it gets its own section.

Okay, let's go over something really simple first: Most people do not like to read anything that is "hard" to read. And, at a glance, there is very little that says "hard to read" quite like a LOT of words all mashed together.

Think about this: Do you remember high school or college? Specifically, English class? Do you remember having to read books and then writing book reports on them? Do you remember how you felt when a 4-inch thick book was assigned (like *A Tale of Two Cities*)? I know how I felt, and it wasn't the happy thoughts of a high school senior. It wasn't even the anxious thought of whether I was going to "get lucky" at one of the many parties I attended (for those wondering, my luck in high school was terrible).

It was more like a thought along the lines of, "Oh man, I'm gonna have to read ALL THAT? It's 4-inches thick! It'll probably take YEARS just to read the ... hey, this thing is heavy ... got some weight to it. I bet if I threw it at Kenny's head, it would hurt. Let's find out ..."

Okay, you get the point. A long, thick book wasn't high on my list (or Kenny's, for that matter). And long paragraphs are not high on your website visitors' lists, either. So shorten them.

Three to five sentences

Ideally, I like my paragraphs to be three to five sentences in length. Sometimes they can be a little longer, but for the most part, three to five is my sweet spot (my general rule is the deeper a visitor gets into your site, the more apt he or she is to put up with longer paragraphs because he or she is interested. Sort of like the nerdy chick and *A Tale of Two Cities*. By the way, I always thought she was cute).

I do realize the general rule of writing is that a paragraph only changes when the thought changes. But to be honest, that's a somewhat arbitrary rule, because it's subject to opinion. In other words, when I think a thought is done, I break the paragraph. Let's do a few examples.

Where would you break the following paragraph?

We do things a little differently here at XYZ Software Development. That's because we are a true custom developer — we do not sell "out of the box" solutions. We instead focus on solving your customer service processing issues by developing software that works for your specific situation. This means the first thing we do is make certain we have a thorough understanding of your unique corporate culture, and are intimately familiar with your people and current processes. This is a key component of what sets us apart from the competition — we feel the solution should fit YOUR way of doing business, not the other way around. By first educating ourselves on how your company does things, we can develop a solution that fits seamlessly with how your people are already working. The result is an effortless software migration, with very little retraining. And the best part is the solution is completely custom-tailored to you.

Personally, I would break it twice. I would break it after the third sentence, and then after the sixth, so it looks like this:

We do things a little differently here at XYZ Software Development. That's because we are a true custom developer — we do not sell "out of the box" solutions. We instead focus on solving your customer service processing issues by developing software that works for your specific situation.

This means the first thing we do is make certain we have a thorough understanding of your unique corporate culture, and are intimately familiar with your people and current processes. This is a key component of what sets us apart from the competition — we feel the solution should fit YOUR way of doing business, not the other way around. By first educating ourselves on how your company does things, we can develop a solution that fits seamlessly with how your people are already working.

The result is an effortless software migration, with very little retraining. And the best part is the solution is completely custom-tailored to you.

Essentially, what I did was take the one general thought and broke it up into a beginning, middle, and end. You don't quite have to do that, but once you pass three sentences in a paragraph, you should be starting to think about the next one and how you are going to get to it.

There's no hard and fast rule I can tell you that will show you without question where to break — you will have to use your own common sense and what sounds right, and/or where a new idea starts. For example, if you are describing, say, a hand truck, you might say:

This hand truck is very strong. That's due to the extra balance provided by the wheels. The left wheel has a built-in stabilizer. The right wheel has special ball bearings, making transporting large loads a breeze. The handle has molded hand grips, for easy grasping. And the lift plate is extra sturdy. Together, these make XYZ the Cadillac® of Hand Trucks.

Can you see the logical break?

Relax, I can't either. There really isn't one. You could perhaps put that last line on its own, but it's not necessary, either. My point is, if the break doesn't make sense to you and seems "off," it probably is.

Let's do another one (no trickery in this next one; there are indeed breaks to be had).

Accounting issues can be all-consuming to a small business. Especially if nobody on staff has the time to educate themselves on the finer points of taxes, balance sheets, payroll, etc. With that in mind, XYZ Accounting specializes in small business accounting on two levels — the end-of-year that all businesses need, and the week-to-week (and even day-to-day) accounting issues that many businesses need help with. In other words, WE can become your accounting department. This means we handle it all — taxes, balance sheets, payroll, and everything else. You simply do what you do best: sell your products and service your customers. We'll handle the rest in an effortless fashion that will make you wonder why you ever tried to handle accounting yourself in the first place. Contact XYZ Accounting today and be amazed at how easy accounting can be.

Personally, I would break this three times. After the second sentence, after the fourth, and after the seventh, so it looks like this:

Accounting issues can be all-consuming to a small business. Especially if nobody on staff has the time to educate themselves on the finer points of taxes, balance sheets, payroll, etc.

With that in mind, XYZ Accounting specializes in small business accounting on two levels — the end-of-year that all businesses need, and the week-to-week (and even day-to-day) accounting issues that many businesses need help with. In other words, WE can become your accounting department.

This means we handle it all — taxes, balance sheets, payroll, and everything else. You simply do what you do best: sell your products and service your customers. We'll handle the rest in an effortless fashion that will make you wonder why you ever tried to handle accounting yourself in the first place.

Contact XYZ Accounting today and be amazed at how easy accounting can be.

See how much easier it is to read?

Now, technically, we didn't HAVE to break it up at all. Many an English teacher would tell us that's one thought. But breaking the one paragraph up into four really drives home the individual points well. Again, use what sounds right to you.

Also, notice what I did with that last line: It REALLY delivers a great call to action (which we'll go over soon. I told you this chapter had lots of intertwining thoughts). That last line (the words "Contact XYZ Accounting Today") can be made a link, and made to seamlessly deliver a reader to your Contact page (or quote form).

It's also a great illustration of one of my favorite paragraph tricks: the one-sentence paragraph.

The one-sentence paragraph

I love one-sentence paragraphs. Used properly, they really make a great call to action (like we just saw); can invite a reader to read further; and also make what I call an effective "paragraph summary."

In short, they can be very useful.

As a call to action

We just saw the "call to action" one-sentence paragraph in the last example. The thought behind that is you can either break it to have a call to action, or just add one. Adding "Start increasing your bottom line and contact XYZ Accounting today" after a paragraph extolling the virtues of XYZ Accounting does no harm whatsoever. Making it a link (even the whole thing) makes it all the better. And you don't have to do this at the end of the page. Quite often I'll ask someone if they'd like to contact me in the middle of a page.

As an introduction

Let's look at my little template page again (the one with the "good" subheadings). Remember this?

Now let me make one teeny little change, as seen in Sample 10.

Much more inviting to start reading, isn't it? The only change I made is I added a few line breaks to make the first sentence of the first paragraph stand on its own (essentially becoming the first paragraph itself). I also use the age-old technique of asking an obvious question (this is a sales copywriting staple — lead off asking the reader the key point you are driving home. It gets the reader in a "yes" frame of mind … I mean, really, who is going to answer "no" to that opening question)?

The one-sentence paragraph starts off your webpage in a very friendly, easy-to-read way. In short, it's rather inviting, and makes things easy right from the start, which really should be a goal of yours. It's like a store — if you make it hard for me to park, I may not come at all. Make it easy, and I'm there. That's why the mall killed downtown; it's not so much that the prices were so much lower (do you really think we comparison shop for a picture frame?), it's that it was more convenient to shop. And it's why the Internet is starting to hurt the mall.

Now, I'm not saying the one-sentence paragraph leading off your site will guarantee traffic, etc. I am saying that it may help make reading easier. And easier is better. You don't need to do it on every page (it becomes silly then), but leading off the site with a one-sentence paragraph is a nice way to invite readers in.

As a paragraph summary

I love to summarize a paragraph by using a one-sentence paragraph right after it that makes a somewhat bold statement, while also giving a reader almost no choice but to agree with what I just wrote. Perhaps that'll be clearer with an example:

SAMPLE 10

ONE-SENTENCE PARAGRAPH LEADING OFF A PAGE

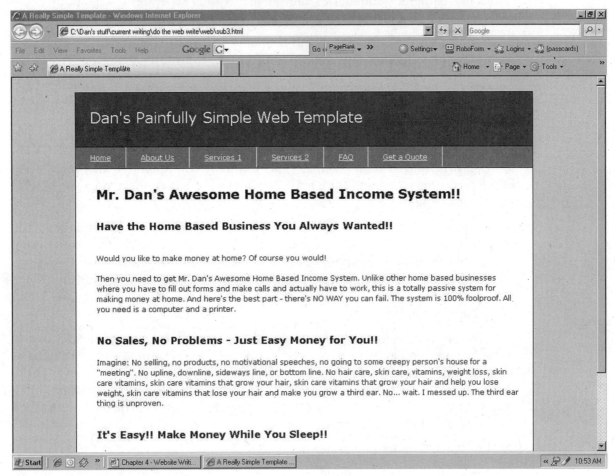

Our accounting software becomes an integral part of your operation, and seamlessly integrates with your proprietary software. This means your people do not need to re-learn how to do their jobs, as your old system is left intact. Combine this with the incredible array of new features our software offers, and you get an immense amount of added functionality, without any additional retraining costs, which adds considerably to your bottom line.

In other words, instead of being an expense, our software MAKES you money.

See what I did? Essentially, I boldly summed up the paragraph with the most salient point. The other added benefit here is that if someone scanned the page, they'd read the "in other words" paragraph FIRST — and isn't that what you'd WANT a reader to take away if they were only going to read one thing?

The paragraph summary is one of my favorite things to use. It's just something I've always done, without ever really realizing it was special. But it is special — doing things like paragraph summaries and the like is what separates a website that converts from one that just kind of sits there.

You can also use the paragraph summary to (sort of) contrast the preceding paragraph, like this (this one comes right from my website):

Exceptional corporate communications and corporate writing will go a long way in making you and/or your company shine. For example, saying just the right thing in tough times can really make a difference, and the positive effects can last for years.

And saying the wrong thing can ruin years of work.

Using the one sentence summary like I do here still reiterates the overall point of the preceding paragraph (hire me!), but does so by extolling the opposite of what I'm talking about.

Also, notice that that line isn't a great sales line like my first example was. You could scan my first example, and come away with an understandable, positive point ("our software makes you money"). But if you scan the second example ("And saying the wrong thing can ruin years of work)," you likely come away with "huh?" On its own, it makes no sense — you HAVE to read the preceding to understand it. But that's okay in this case.

See, this copy is from an "interior" page on my site (meaning a reader had to navigate here from another page), so I'm not quite as concerned about scanning as I am on other pages (after all, if they weren't interested in me, they'd never get to this page in the first place). Instead of "scanning" (which is still important, mind you, but maybe not quite as much as other pages), I'm just a little more concerned with selling and making a point.

Let's do one more paragraph summary:

Crash McRickety's Home Improvement has been serving the Mooseville area for over 30 years. This longevity is no accident; we've remained a leader in our industry due to our attention to detail, the high quality of our work, and the complete satisfaction of our clients. And not only are we exceptional at home improvement, but we show up on time, are reasonably priced, and we stay until the job is finished.

In other words, we're everything you could ever want in a home improvement contractor. Contact us today.

Yes, I cheated — that's a two sentence summary. But that's fine — calls to action are always good. Plus, I've said over and over that none of these rules are hard and fast. By the way, that passage was obviously in jest (although it still remains an excellent example of the summary) — if you are a contractor, try and avoid using the word "accident" in your advertising. Doubly so if your first name is Crash.

Rule 3: Don't Dwell (Keep Your Pages Short)

Most webpages are too long. Obviously, I'm not talking about those one-page sales letter-style pages (those are supposed to be really long), but I am talking about regular product and service sites. There is just way too much information on the pages, and many times, a visitor can easily get lost, become confused, and/or just give up. So Rule 3 is simple: shorter pages, and don't dwell.

There are two points to this rule: formatting and content style. Let's do formatting first.

Formatting

In keeping with the "shorter is better" theme of the last rule, I'm going to extend that to your pages as well. Just like the thickness of a textbook has an adverse affect on many, that scrollbar on the right side of the web browser getting really small elicits the same type of negative response. It says, "Here's a really long page with lots of reading — pour some coffee, because you're going to need it." (Okay, it doesn't say quite that. It doesn't really know if you even LIKE coffee. You might like tea. Or one of those specialty drinks from the coffee place that takes the counter person NINE YEARS to make while you patiently wait to order a very simple large coffee … listen Mr. 155-pound, angsty arteest with your laptop full of lousy poetry, could you possibly make your order any MORE annoying? "Okay, I want the large double-mocha frappuccino with the extra frothy top — 2% please, I'm on a diet — with chocolate shavings and light whipped cream. Oh, could I get that with a half shot of coconut syrup and a half shot of butter rum too, but do the butter rum after you mix it up.")

That's about the time the really evil (and messy) thoughts come to my mind.

I'm sorry, but these places really need two lines: one for people ordering coffee, and one for self-important people ordering annoyingly complicated drinks. Anyway, I apologize for getting off track, but it had to be said. My point still remains. Really long pages aren't viewed favorably by most web surfers.

In short, the longer the page, the worse the initial reaction will be. And the worse your sales and contacts will be.

In fact, there have been studies done that suggest most web surfers won't even scroll a little bit on a page unless it first interests them. This means anything below the bottom of the web browser might not ever be seen (and the size varies; monitor size and screen resolution all play a part).

Now, I am not suggesting that all of your pages be the size of a web browser; that is impractical (none of mine are). However, there's no reason why your very best points can't be as high up on the page as possible. Generally, I like to try and make sure most viewers will see at least one to two subheadings without scrolling (or one subheading and some bullets, perhaps). This also means a picture that takes up half the screen is out. Why otherwise-smart companies do that, I'll never know.

I personally like to keep the pages small enough so the scrollbar doesn't get really small — generally, I look to go no bigger than double the screen size. In other words, I want the average person to see at least half the page without scrolling. Now, like everything else, this isn't hard and fast. The "deeper" into your site someone goes, the longer your pages can be (because obviously, the reader is then interested). But I don't want anyone to feel intimidated by my site — my site says "I'm friendly, easy to read, and I'm not a lot of work." My site is the large coffee of the Internet — I let someone else be the annoying "venti, non-fat, extra hot macchiato, no whip, extra caramel … " (Note to the people that order these: The rest of us HATE you. Okay, I'll get off the coffee shop thing now).

Quote from Anywhere

This "most people don't scroll" thing is one reason why having a link to your Quote page on your main navigation is important. Do NOT make it so people have to scroll to contact you — put a quote (or contact) button right on the link bar. You can even put your phone number on the top or the side of every page (which I do and it works nicely).

Then, also somewhere in the middle of the page, put a text link to your Quote page (ideally in the paragraph summary that you learned to do earlier). The general idea here is to ALWAYS have a way to get to your Quote page (or Buy/Purchase/Cart page) in front of the visitor. I mean at all times. NEVER leave anyone searching for how to contact you (or buy from you).

Content style

Now we'll discuss content style, the second part of Rule 3.

Real quick — what is the main purpose of a résumé?

If you answered, "To get you a job," well, you're wrong. If you answered, "To get you an interview," you're closer to being right, but you are still sort of wrong (aren't I making you feel wonderful)?

A résumé serves two purposes. The first, and most important, purpose of a résumé is not to get you a job, or even an interview. It's to get you the contact (phone call, email) that leads to an interview. The second purpose is to be a supporting reference once that interview is held (so the interviewer can say "I see here you fixed the loose handles on highway rest area bathroom stalls … impressive … we can definitely use you on the space shuttle program").

You can look at most business websites in the same way: The overriding goal is to get a contact (or an order), and the rest of the site is there for supporting purposes. So, like I've been saying, your website needs to be geared towards doing this. And that means you do not need to dwell on and on about your company.

Most business owners feel the need to dwell, unfortunately. I know I did in the beginning. I felt there was SO MUCH I needed to tell my visitors about me and my service. I was forgetting one of the golden rules of sales: Say what you need to say, ask for the order, and then SHUT UP. In fact, in sales, they tell you the first person to speak after a "close" loses.

Your website needs to be the same way. You need to tell enough to get someone interested in contacting you, ask them to contact you, and then you kind of need to shut up. If you feel the need to say something else, do so on another page.

For example, I've seen websites where on the Services page the services are listed, and then the company goes into all the reasons to do business with them — it goes on and on about years in business, the guarantee, etc., but shouldn't that stuff be on the About Us page? A properly set up website (preferably somewhat following what I outlined in Chapter 3) will give you plenty of opportunity to exalt the benefits you offer, without the extra information getting in the way.

Like I already mentioned, my general rule is to be twice the normal screen size (and what screen size is normal? Mine, of course!) If you feel you have more to say, and it's going to take up some room, you can always make another page (and using the flyout method mentioned earlier if linking, you can add a LOT of links / pages without cluttering everything up).

To give you a good example of this, I once felt I should let people know my work process and what to expect when they hired me. At first, I put this on my main services page. It was about four paragraphs of text, and really made the page too long.

I noticed a marked decline in contacts from this page. I surmised that people all of a sudden saw that it was a long page and just didn't bother with it. So I took that stuff down and put it on a new page called Our Work Process (and put the link under a resources flyout). Immediately, the contacts from my services page rose again (and those who were interested visited the Process page as well).

> Okay, stop right there, Dan. Do you mean to tell me that something as silly as the page being longer will turn a person who is interested into someone who leaves? I'm sorry, but I refuse to believe that people are THAT picky. I mean, I never went to a page and said, "This is too long … I gotta leave."
>
> Yes, that is EXACTLY what I am telling you. And yes, I'm sure you never said that to yourself when you saw a really long page — you probably just left. You don't even know WHY you left. You just did. In general terms, long webpages DON'T work. It doesn't matter if you (or anyone else) personally doesn't see the connection (or disconnection, to be more accurate) — for most sites, long pages make people leave (again, sales letter websites excepted).

Trust me here, I found out the hard way that saying too much is usually not good. But this is a common thing, and hard to overcome sometimes (you often need to be told to tone things down). One thing business owners and high level corporate people have in common is they love their company and/or products. And not only do they love their company, they are convinced they can help you, and they want to cover every single angle of such. I can empathize because again, I did just that.

Bottom line: Say what you need to say to get a contact, then shut up. And I mean that in the nicest possible way (look, I'm even smiling as I type)!

But what about stickiness? Don't you need long pages for that?

Having a sticky website (one that people stay at a long time and return to) used to be a big deal. I personally don't think it's that big a deal — in fact, I think it's overrated (and I've got a REAL sticky site … ew. That doesn't sound right. Sorry). Truth be told, I really don't care how long people stay around. I care if they contact me. If staying around longer makes them more apt to contact me, great. But I have found that hasn't been the case; the average person who contacts me spends less than 2 minutes on my site.

Having stickiness without contacts and/or sales might be a badge of honor, or make you feel good, but it's not ideal — contacts and/or sales are better. Still, I won't deny that having stickiness means something. If you find you have good stickiness (which I would define as one and a half minutes or more for an average visit), it means that you are at least interesting to people. So test other things (Quote page, links) and find out where the issue is. Oh, and test them one at a time too — much easier to keep track of things that way.

SAMPLE 11
ANCHOR LINKS EXAMPLE

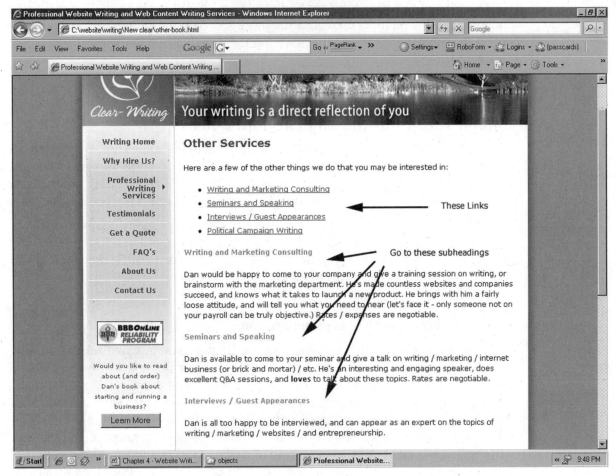

But what if I really need to have a long page?

Okay, sometimes a longer page is seemingly unavoidable. Assuming you will follow other things I outline in this book (short paragraphs, subheadings, etc.), there are two ways you can overcome a longer page.

1. **Use a bulleted list up top that anchor links to text below:** This allows visitors to browse what's on the page, click the thing that interests them the most, and be taken right to it, without leaving the page. And if you don't understand what an anchor link is, it's a link within the same page (just ask your web person to do it).

2. **Use subheadings, and provide a Get a Quote link (or the like) after each paragraph/service:** But I much prefer method one if you need a long page

with lots of services. Sample 11 is an example from my site (the page isn't terribly long, but it's a good example of anchor links).

I shortened this page a bit for Sample 11 so I could get both the list and three anchors all in the picture (there's a little more space on the actual page — you can't see all the subheadings when you view it on the web, hence making the anchor links necessary).

Okay, we're done with Rule 3. Keep your pages short. Let's move on.

Rule 4: Throw Out the English Rule Book

Okay, you've probably noticed that the rules are changing somewhat. We started off with strict formatting, and now we're starting to get a little more into grammar and writing "style." And there's no better way to kick that off than by telling you that yes, you can fulfill a childhood fantasy and chuck out your English textbook.

I am convinced that trying to write right is what keeps many people from writing well (that's a rather odd sentence, isn't it? Read it again if you have to). People just get so wound up in making sure their grammar is correct that they let it get in the way of just writing what they mean.

I'm here to tell you that it's okay.

Let me make a small confession: two confessions, actually.

The first confession is that in high school, English was my worst subject. Really, I was terrible. And one of the reasons I was terrible was because I just wrote what I meant, and not to the standards of perfect English. I just didn't know all the rules, and never really cared to learn them. And it seemed (to me, anyway) that high school English was more concerned with making me memorize the stupid rules than it was with getting interesting writing from me. Because, you know, I could always write well. I got great marks on any kind of writing I did as a kid — heaps of praise. But then as I got older, the praise stopped and I got a lot of red Xs, along with comments like, "That's not a complete thought," or "Stop with the dashes already," or my favorite, which was "See me after class." In fact, my high school English work had so many red marks you'd think I bled on it.

The second confession I want to make is that while I make my living as a professional writer, I still truly do not know many rules of English (probably no more than you do). For example, for the life of me, I do not know what a preposition is (I'm not kidding). And I have long forgotten what a pronoun is.

And you know what? It doesn't matter. I don't need to know them. Besides, I'm WAY too busy making sure people's websites are read and understood (and writing books on the side) than to be concerned with if my writing would get a good mark.

Which brings me to this ...

The way we are taught to write is wrong (for business)

Like I previously mentioned, we already get handicapped because we are worried about the rules and such. But let's look at some other things I feel are wrong with how we are taught to write:

- According to most teachers I have had, short paragraphs are out. Long paragraphs are in. This is how they tried to teach me (which I ignored, hence the bad marks), and it's DEAD WRONG in regards to business writing (which includes website copy). Like we went over, the shorter your paragraphs are, the easier they are to read. And we already know that's good.

- Many times, you are told almost all writing needs a thesis statement (an opening statement that says what the writing/page is about). That's wonderful for book reports and perhaps white papers. It's awful for web copy.

- We get taught a lot of formatting and the like. Just not the right formatting for the web. Nobody told me about subheadings and bullet points. However, I was taught to indent new paragraphs in school (and endlessly chastised for not doing it). And to this day, I still see paragraphs indented online. Stop — it looks ridiculous on a website. It's fine in a book, and that's about it (note: I didn't indent the manuscript because I don't write that way; all indents are editor-inspired).

- You are not allowed to break form or structure in school. Inserting an aside in parentheses (like this) or a subheading somewhere is almost always forbidden, and results in a bad mark (trust me, I know). But to me, breaking form in web copy is oftentimes GOOD. Inserting a Contact Us link after a paragraph telling the reader how you can help them is usually GOOD.

- In school, you are also almost always taught to write in first person (I) or third person (they). You are almost never taught to write in second person (you). Yet a mixture of the three, with the biggest emphasis on second, is the best form of website writing. Rule 8 gets deeper into this subject.

How many rules does your reader know?

One other reason following the more obscure rules of English don't really matter is the fact that aside from English teachers, nobody really knows them anyway. Do you really think your reader can spot a fragment? The odds are overwhelming that they might not. So, knowing that, if your writing is interesting and clear, does it really matter if it has fragments nobody knows about? Trust me, in regards to business, it really doesn't.

Write like you talk

One simple way around the whole "am I doing this right?" aspect is to simply write like you talk. When you write something, say it out loud. Does it sound natural? Or does it sound robotic and/or forced? If it sounds anything but natural, it's wrong for your website, regardless of grammar and the like. It should flow naturally from your lips, almost sounding like something you would say.

This means when you write something, say out loud what you just wrote (including all pauses for the punctuation you used). If it doesn't sound natural to you, change it until it does. Repeat the process; keep saying out loud what you wrote, and experiment until what you wrote sounds natural. Yes, it's a little more work to do things this way, but it will make your overall writing a LOT better. If it sounds good to your EARS, it will probably read well to your audience's EYES.

But What about Dictation Software?

This brings me to an interesting dilemma — if I want you to write like you talk, and I want it to sound like something you would say, what about dictating and the like?

While it sounds good in theory, I have found it doesn't work well at all. I've tried it with voice recognition software and the like, and the results have been subpar at best (and I don't mean in the function of the software, which worked fine). I can't put my finger on it, but there's a definite difference between writing the words, and saying the words. Writing like you talk does not mean talking to write.

I wish I could explain this better, but it's one of those "it's just not quite right" things. But take it from this writer: dictation software does not equal good writing (there goes my million-dollar endorsement contract)!

Okay, so what rules of English do you need to know?

I don't want to sound like I advocate bad grammar. I don't. I just think over-worrying about obscure rules is silly. But I'd be lying if I didn't say that there are some rules you MUST follow. Here they are:

- ✏ Capitalize words that should be capitalized. That means names, etc., and the start of a sentence.

- ✏ For the most part, use proper basic punctuation. If you ask a question, use a question mark. If you want some emphasis, use an exclamation point. Use commas where there should be a slight pause. If you aren't sure whether a comma should go somewhere or not, say the sentence out loud like you intend it to be read. If a pause sounds good to you, then put a comma in (or a dash — that's why I say for the most part. More on formatting in Rule 9).

✏ You have to spell correctly, and you have to use the RIGHT words. For example, you can't say "loose" when you mean "lose" (this is an astonishingly common mistake. A good way to remember the proper uses of these is to commit the following sentence to memory: "Team A knocked the ball loose, which made Team B lose the game.")

I can't think of many more than that in regards to what you need to know in as far as rules of the English language. Perhaps an English teacher out there can help me some here (after he or she gets done sticking pins in the Dan doll).

And since I just mentioned the "loose" and "lose" thing, let's take a second and expand on a few more commonly misspelled words and misused phrases.

Commonly misspelled words and misused phrases

To, Two, and Too: I am going TO the store to buy TWO pieces of candy — I hope it doesn't cost TOO much. "I want TO go, TOO," said Eileen.

Principal, Principle: The Principal suspended him on principle. Also, remember that the principal is the main person in a school (and therefore gets an A. Get it?) And since he or she is the main person in a school, almost any "main" thing can be called a principal (the principal reason I am suspending you … the company principals voted to merge).

Than, Then: "Then" is generally a period of time ("I'll do it then"). "Than" is generally a comparison ("bigger than"). In other words, one thing is NEVER "bigger then" another.

It's, Its: This one is simple — "it's" is short for "it is". If "it is" doesn't work in the sentence, then it's "its."

There, Their, They're: "There" is a place, "their" is possessive, and "they're" is "they are". They're moving their stuff over there.

Could care less / Couldn't care less: Another one that drives me insane. The proper phrase is "couldn't care less." "Could care less" makes no sense at all in the context that this phrase is always used. Think about it.

These are only a few, but they are the most glaring errors I see. Learn these few and your writing will be a lot better.

In closing

There's not much more I can say about this rule. The rule is to generally ignore the more obscure rules of English.

And let me mention it one more time to make you feel confident even if you don't know the rules of English — I'm a professional writer. One who gets paid to write by businesses, and one whose writing makes people money. I even write books, and I don't know these rules. Now if I can do this without knowing proper English, how important do you think it really is in regards to website copy?

Rules are definitely getting shorter. Let's go to Rule 5.

Rule 5: Do Not Preach to the Choir

This rule is more geared towards service-oriented websites (although it has some merit for product-oriented sites too).

I remember a big mistake I made when I first launched my professional writing website. I preached to the choir — big time. And it cost me a lot of business.

Here's what I did: As I mentioned in Rule 3, there was just SO much I wanted to tell my website visitors. And one of the things that I really wanted to hammer was to explain — in detail — exactly WHY my visitor needed a professional writer. In fact, I thought that was a really important thing to do. I wanted to get my visitor to say, "Yes, I really NEED a writer."

So I led off my website outlining the reasons one would need a professional writer, and then talked about the benefits a professional writer offered: How a professional writer makes your copy convert better, how a professional writer makes your ideas clear, etc. Pretty much led off my website with four paragraphs of this stuff.

However, I was forgetting something very important. Like millions of other sites, I get the majority of my traffic from search engines and the like, and my site typically comes up when one searches for some type of writer.

Therefore, since the overwhelming majority of the people coming to my site searched for some type of writer, they kind of already made the decision to hire a writer, didn't they? They didn't say to themselves, "Let me search for a way to make my website clearer," they said, "Let me find a writer." And boom, they found my site.

In other words, because they actually searched for a writer, THEY ALREADY DECIDED THEY NEEDED A WRITER. If they didn't decide that, they never would have searched for one in the first place. They would have instead searched for garbage can deodorizer or a new oven mitt (or whatever else they were looking for).

So, knowing that my visitor already decided he or she needed a writer's help, isn't it sort of a waste for me to spend time going over WHY, and instead I should go over the reasons why I'M the writer needed?

This is really a "duh" moment, but it's one of the biggest mistakes people make online. They try to sell their overall industry instead of selling themselves.

I recall rewriting a website for an accountant. He had a small site (perhaps five pages), but four of those pages largely talked about the benefits that a professional accountant can bring you. ANY professional accountant. The site converted at about 1%.

I rewrote it to instead focus on the company itself and why a visitor should hire THIS accountant. My copy assumed that the visitor already wanted to hire an accountant (after all, why were they searching for one?), and addressed the reasons my client was the best choice. Bottom line, I quadrupled his conversions to 4% — essentially, I grew his online business four-fold.

Targeted traffic revisited

Are you beginning to see how a lot of what I am talking about ties together? Here I am mentioning not preaching to the choir, and we're back to knowing where your visitor came from. I can't predict with 100% accuracy what is going through my visitor's head, but by knowing the search terms the majority of visitors are using, I can definitely predict their general mindset when they come to my site. If they search for any type of "writer," I have to assume they already thought along the lines of "I think I need a writer."

Does that make sense to you? Can you see how having targeted traffic pays off in more ways than one? If you know what terms your visitor is using, you can get an idea of WHY they are coming, and you can then tailor your website to address those reasons.

I mentioned earlier that this rule is more geared towards service-oriented websites and businesses. This is because generally, I find that service businesses, for some reason, feel the need to sell the service first, and themselves second. Which is okay for some situations, but is backwards online. Online, if someone searches for a service, they almost certainly already decided they need some form of that service. No need to sell them on the service when they get to your site. Sell them on you.

Now, I'm not advocating totally ignoring the "sell the industry" angle. I indeed eventually mention how a professional writer can help you on my website. But it's buried pretty deep; I'm WAY more interested in talking about how MY BUSINESS can HELP YOU.

What's your problem?

A simple way to remember to not preach to the choir is to remember that most visitors come to your website with some sort of problem, and it is your job to solve that problem for them. And again, this is especially true (almost universally so) with service-based websites. They came to you with a problem that your service can solve, SO SOLVE THEIR PROBLEM FOR THEM.

Say you are a plumber. Leading your website off with: *"Are you looking for a plumber in the Anytown area? Then you came to the right place. At Drain Odor Plumbing, we service any plumbing need you may have. From installations to emergency repairs to new construction, we do it all"* totally and completely solves the problem that 99% of visitors have. They are looking for a plumber in Anytown for some reason, and boy did they find one.

Now again, this seems very obvious, but it really isn't. For example, I cannot count the number of plumbing (etc.) sites that right away went into something like this:

"If you need a plumber in Anytown, you need to choose a licensed professional over the handyman type. That's because only a licensed professional has the knowledge it takes to properly service your home's plumbing. Yes, a licensed professional may cost a little more than a handyman, but the quality of service is unparalleled."

In other words, this guy is trying to tell you that choosing a real plumber over a cheaper-priced handyman is best. This might make a nice argument somewhere on the About Us page, but it's not appropriate for leading off the site. In all honesty, most people would leave after reading the above paragraph because it doesn't solve a problem. Instead, it almost picks a fight.

Yes, you read that correctly. In all honesty, the preceding is somewhat akin to picking a fight. That's because it assumes an argument that may not even be in your reader's mind. Yes, I realize many professional, licensed tradespeople (or anyone, really) do not like losing out to lower-priced, less skilled, inferior businesses, but why assume everyone is thinking along that line? Why even bring it up? It's pointless, and detracts from what's most important: selling YOUR company.

To give you another example that hits close to home for me, I don't like losing business to cheap copywriters from India who charge $5 a page, but I'm not going to start that argument on my home page — I'm instead going to tell you that I handle all manner of professional writing, and here's exactly what my writing can do for you. I won't get into why a professional is better than a non-professional or the like. It's boring, and it's counterproductive.

What are they expecting from you?

This is a recurring theme with me, but besides having some kind of problem, your visitor definitely has an expectation for your website. In the case of the plumber, I want to know that my plumbing problems will be solved, that he or she is local, and that he or she will come fast. Meet these expectations and your site will generally succeed (by the way, I use plumbing a lot in my examples because it's a very easy example for anyone to relate to. Everyone knows there are plumbers out there, and why people need them. So it's an easily understood example, hence my using it over and over. I'd use my own business more often, but many out there can't relate to it. I still have friends that cannot believe I make a living writing for companies. They cannot fathom why anyone would need me).

Okay, pretty easy rule, right? Remember why your audience is there, and address the issues that brought them to you. And in doing so, sell them on YOU, not your industry. Which brings me to Rule 6.

Rule 6: Keep Your Audience in Mind, but Don't Alienate Anyone, Either

This rule is twofold, and both sides are somewhat contradictory to each other. You must write so your audience understands and relates to you, but at the same time, you can't go alienating people with insider jargon. Let's do these one at a time.

Write so your audience understands you

You need to write in terms that your audience will understand (and, to a point, relate to). For example, say you have a website selling a skateboard. Depending on your audience, you could generally go about writing your site one of two ways.

If your aim is to sell to retailers, then you are selling to the adults that handle product acquisition. By all means, discuss the superior quality of the high precision all-steel ball-bearing wheel casings that produce an above-average product lifespan, resulting in fewer returns and higher product margins at the point of sale. Retail people get all excited over margins and such (indeed, the centerfold of *Modern Retailer* is always a spreadsheet).

But if your aim is to sell directly to the end user (which is mainly teenage boys), then you probably want to say that this skateboard can take a serious beating and still come back for more. Yes, it's a bit more expensive, but it's worth every penny (and if you can throw a hot girl in there somewhere, all the better).

The lesson here is you have to take your general audience into consideration and write in terms they understand. The corporate buyer will be put off if you don't talk something like a businessperson. And the teenager will be put off if you mention product margins (although less so if you follow the hot girl rule … Having been a teenage boy once, I can tell you firsthand that they are VERY susceptible to the hot girl method of marketing. Okay, I'll admit it … at 42, I'm still pretty vulnerable to this).

So use terms your audience will understand. If you are selling to high-end businesspeople, using words and phrases like "margin," "financial infrastructure," "ROI," "business processes," "legacy systems," etc., might be expected. I have done websites for companies that only serviced very high-end companies. If the reader didn't know what a legacy system was, they weren't a customer anyway ... in that case, it was okay to use these high level terms.

In other words, speak like your audience speaks.

Now let's contradict what I just wrote...

Don't alienate anyone

However (and here's where the contradiction lies), most businesses are not so tightly focused in their client base. Thus, you cannot alienate anyone by using too much insider jargon, or assume your entire audience knows what you are talking about. If you use the term "ROI" by itself, you need to be almost certain that almost your entire reading audience knows what it means. Because if someone doesn't know what it means, and you don't explain what it means, you definitely lost a potential customer.

This happens a lot; when someone too close to the company writes the copy, they often use insider terms that they understand, but a client may not. I did it myself in this book: I said way back in the introduction that I write "copy." Of course, right away, I explained what copy means in this regard, but if I didn't explain it right then and there, would you know what I was talking about? Really, did you know that marketing people, advertisers, and writers often refer to writing as copy? If you did, that's great, but if you didn't, don't feel bad. One of my college English professors didn't know this either. Nor did my sister, who owns a very successful jewelry store. Truth be told, MANY businesspeople don't know "copy" equals "writing" (I could really confuse you now by saying I'm a "copywriter," but I won't).

My point is, I would be doing myself (and my readers) a disservice if I did not explain what I meant and just assumed everyone knew what I was talking about. This means you cannot use insider terms unless you are completely confident that almost all of your readers will know exactly what you are talking about.

Dancing between the two

Okay, I just told you to use language your readers expect. I also told you not to alienate anyone. This is a delicate issue that seems to have no clear answer. So, how do we solve this contradiction I just gave you?

I admit, dancing between the two rules is often necessary. Take me, for example: My business serves corporate clients, and it serves small businesses too. I need to speak to both.

Thus, to satisfy the corporate end, I really need to use the term "ROI" on my website. Corporate marketing people (which comprise a good chunk of my client base) know and understand this term, and sort of expect it.

EXPLAINING INSIDER JARGON

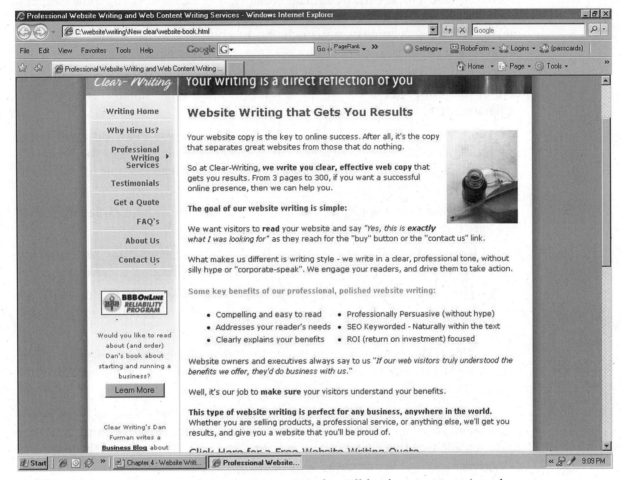

But at the same time, many entrepreneurs and small-business owners (another good chunk of my client base) do not know what it means, and might say, "Huh?" (by the way, it means "Return on Investment." If I say my writing is "ROI focused," it means my aim is to make them money).

So what do I do in this case? Simple.

I use the term, and also explain it in the same sentence. I say my writing is "ROI (Return on Investment) focused." This way, I get the term in, and I explain it as well.

This has two positive effects: It satisfies both parties, and it also makes the person who didn't know what it meant feel like he or she learned something. It's not much; just a tiny little positive feeling, like the feeling one gets when you have exactly 11 cents in change in your pocket and your purchase rings up to $22.11 (woo hoo)! That's always good.

Conversely, NOT explaining the term to someone who doesn't know it has the opposite effect. It's a slight negative feeling, like when your purchase rings up to 23.06, you have a nickel, the penny cup is empty, and the expression on the cashier's face basically says, "The guy before you was a HUGE jerk, my significant other left me, my brother is sleeping on my couch next to a bottle of whiskey, and my car died. So YOU'RE gonna pay. Here's your 94 cents … oh, and have a nice day."

So if you feel the need to use insider jargon or high-level terms, and you are not certain your entire audience will know what they mean, the simplest solution is to explain the term right then and there.

Another way around explaining insider jargon is to use many different terms that mean the same thing. In other words, you don't explain it, but by the sheer volume of other terms and writing, it's obvious what you mean. Sample 12 will make things a little clearer.

Notice what I am doing in the example. I say web copy without explaining it. But there are three things working in my favor here:

1. This is an inside page on my site. In other words, many came here from my home page — thus, they already know I offer writing.

2. However, this is also a landing page (meaning a Google ad directly links to it — more on landing pages in Chapter 9). But the ad discusses writing. So again, they know I offer writing.

3. This is the most important point. I use many terms interchangeably (good for SEO), and use "website writing" in the headline and in the next two subheadings. So it's very obvious that "copy" equals writing.

Now, all that said, I am sure that I still lose a few people because "copy" confused them. However, I lost MORE people when I explained what "copy" was because it made that first sentence too awkward. It used to say, "Your website writing (sometimes referred to as website copy) is the key to online success … " Sometimes, making your leading sentence awkward isn't good. In simple terms, I found that MORE people contacted me once I shortened that first sentence and took out the explanation.

So, even though I said earlier that explaining is good, well, sometimes it isn't (are you beginning to see why website copy is not an exact science, and why testing is so important?)

Now I do not mean to contradict myself here or have this fuzzy grey line on purpose. What I am trying to get across is the fact that you need to TEST and take these tidbits that I am giving you and work them into your own situation. If you are using insider terms, try and explain them in your copy. Give it a solid month, and record the numbers. Then change things; do the "overkill / obvious" route next (like I did in the picture). Give that a solid month, and record the results. Go with the one that gave you better results (of course, this assumes an "apples-to-apples" test. A pool company testing in the middle of winter might not get the most qualified traffic with which to test).

Lose the corporate jargon, again

Okay, let's talk (again) about overly corporate writing. It's gotten to a point where it's ridiculous. If I see one more company that offers "results-based dynamic solutions focused on positive growth across multiple business paradigms," I'm going to throw up.

Listen very carefully: If an average high school graduate cannot figure out what you are saying, then your website copy is too complicated. I know you may not be selling to high schoolers, but if your copy needs a six-year degree to understand it, you will lose business. Take it from me. I write copy for some really big companies with millions of dollars in revenue, and I do so in fairly plain language. I do not use words and/or phrases like "paradigm," "solutions-based," "team empowerment," etc.

I have also been around many a corporate bigwig. Trust me when I tell you, NONE of them talk that way. I have never once heard the word "paradigm" spoken by a person in normal conversation. I have also never heard the phrase "solutions-based" come out of a person's mouth. People do NOT talk like that, so don't write like that.

There is definitely a way to look and sound professional without resorting to corporate jargon. Saying, "Our services result in millions of dollars saved" is better than saying, "We offer dynamic solutions which positively impact your overall financial composition." And yes, it's better to write in simple terms even if you are a huge company.

Trust me here: There's a reason corporate jargon is made fun of, and a reason I felt compelled to state it again. Don't use it. Just write what you mean.

Rule 7: Write with Confidence

One thing that I feel really sets me apart from other writers is that I write with a lot of confidence. When you write with confidence, it almost forces people to agree with you, which can be extremely effective in business writing and website copy (and any writing, really).

I know this is Rule 7, and within each rule I said it was important — and indeed, Rule 1 is most important when it comes to web copy — but personally, if I could only use one of my rules for the rest of my life, I'd use this one.

In short, writing with confidence has gotten me through life, to be honest. If you can write with confidence, you can sound like an authority on almost anything, without really being one. I wrote (or BS'd, depending on who you asked) my way into jobs, into good grades on papers, etc., all because I wrote with confidence. It's EX-TREMELY powerful, and it's deceptively simple to learn how to do, too.

I already showed you how to do one trick in regards to writing with confidence. Do you remember what it was? Way back in Rule 2, I talked about the paragraph summary, and how making a bold, one-sentence/one-paragraph summary after a piece of text reinforces it.

For example:

"Masochist brand Leaf Blowers have been designed to conform to local noise ordi-nances by a single decibel, ensuring the utmost blowing power while providing maxi-mum irritation for those within 1,000 feet of your home. They have also been designed to phonically utilize morning dew, making this leaf blower an ideal tool for those who wish for everyone around them to realize the benefits of rising early, whether they intended to or not.

In other words, you'll clear leaves, and make sure everyone else is up to tackle the day, all at the same time."

Essentially, the one-paragraph summary sums things up, and reinforces the most important points (blowing leaves and ensuring Dan doesn't oversleep).

But I did something else in the main paragraph, too. Can you see it? I essentially said that this leaf blower is "an ideal tool for those who ... "

In other words, I didn't let the reader decide if this was an ideal tool for him or her — I simply went ahead and stated that it was. There is simply no choice in the matter for the reader.

When I write, I try to add one of these reinforcing statements every second or third paragraph or so. Either by a paragraph summary, a reinforcing statement, or both.

Writing with confidence allows you to almost become a buddy with the reader and bring them along with you. When you use many of the confident words and phrases I am going to show you, it helps you sound more like a "person," and it is also far more interesting for the reader.

Confident words and phrases

Okay, there are many ways to write with confidence. You will discover some on your own, but let me start you off here with a few:

- ▭ Now
- ▭ Okay
- ▭ Essentially

- So
- In other words
- In short

About these words and others like them, have you noticed how many times I lead off a sentence with one of these words or phrases? My goodness, I must have done it 100 times already in this book. Doing this does two things; it sounds VERY confident, and it also fits in with the "write like you talk" thing I advocate. This is a good place to begin with confident writing, because it's very simple to implement. Consciously try and start a few sentences off with phrases like this. Work them in so it sounds natural.

In addition (hey, there's another one), when you use words and phrases like these, your writing becomes FAR more interesting to the reader. It's hard to resist reading a sentence that starts off with, "Now … " (and yeah, use the ellipsis [three dots] too, if you wish).

Many of these phrases are great for the summary paragraph, as well. "Essentially" or "in other words" are great lead-ins to your bold one-sentence summary (in fact, they somewhat define the summary). They also offer little wiggle room (the reader almost HAS to believe what you just wrote, even if he or she isn't 100% sure about it). Now, I'm not saying lie and then cover it up with a confident summary; that's dishonest, and I do not advocate that in the least. However, a summary can make an honest claim (or a product feature, etc.), seem like an undisputed fact in the reader's mind.

By the way, the "however" I just used is another good one. Not quite as strong as the others, but stronger than nothing.

"Obviously" and "clearly" are two very powerful confidence words. Because they carry such weight, I use them sparingly. But when you bring them out, it's like bringing in the big guns. Like this:

"Our software integrates seamlessly with your existing systems. Obviously, this is a huge advantage to you, and clearly sets us apart from the competition. "

These words not only give the reader no choice but to agree with you, they take it one step further by essentially saying "you would be stupid to disagree." Because, clearly, anyone can see that you know what you are talking about (see what I mean)? By the way, I usually don't use both together like I just did in the example (but I have to admit, it does work nicely there).

Using words like this every so often builds credibility. It makes the whole of your writing that much more believable. And it works online or off (I'm sure you realize by now that everything I am teaching you carries weight in the offline world as well).

To give you an example I remember well, I recall a Civil War paper I wrote when I went to college. I was going through the list of top Union generals during the first few years of the war (Scott, McClellan, Burnside, Hooker, etc.), and used the phrase "Clearly, neither could convince Lincoln that he was capable of total victory against the Rebels." The professor (this was a 300-level Civil War class) commented very positively on that particular line, and I got an A.

There's a reason I am telling you this — it was at that moment that I had a revelation — I realized he commented on that particular line because it was so confident. Just by using the word "clearly," I said (in unspoken terms) that I really put a lot of research into this paper, and a lot of thought into the claim. It made almost everything I said afterwards shine just a little brighter.

Now here's the funny thing: The actual line touts a pretty pedestrian fact (as you Civil War buffs already know). You do not have to do much research at all on the Civil War to uncover the fact that Lincoln was dissatisfied with his generals (until Grant … okay, enough with the history lesson … back to writing). But the most common and obvious of all facts got the best comment from the professor; not because of the fact, but because of the confidence I put behind it.

I had always written this way, but I never realized what I was doing until that moment. Out of all six pages and perhaps ten comments, he commented the strongest on that particular line. It really made an impression on me, and I went about making certain that ANY writing I did sounded confident.

Now, I won't kid you. I got a good grade because it was a good paper, not because of that one line. But did my confident nature in regards to writing style perhaps bring it from a B+ to an A? I am almost certain it did. And maybe, just maybe, that line put a little plus sign in his head in regards to my work, and perhaps made everything that came after it just seem a teeny bit more credible. That's really the whole secret to good writing (online or off). It's about reinforcing positive thoughts in your reader's head, and making them agree with you.

I've likely already said this, but this one little thing I just taught you — this one itsy-bitsy little tidbit — can reap HUGE benefits for you. Not just online, but in your entire life. Being able to write with confidence has made my life infinitely better, and with a little practice, you can start becoming a more confident writer almost right away. And it's REALLY simple. Start using the confident words and phrases I just taught you, discover a few more on your own, and go where they lead you. You'll soon notice a difference in how you feel about your writing, and also how people react to it.

Got it? Good, let's go to Rule 8.

Rule 8: Use the Word "You" a Lot

If you ask marketing students or advertisers what the most important word in business marketing is, they'll probably say something like "free" or "sale" or whatnot. They would be wrong. The most important word in the English language in terms of business writing is the word "you."

You? Yes, you. Not me, not I, but you.

This fact is somewhat surprising to a lot of people; in fact, most don't even give the word "you" a second thought. But that's a big mistake. If you don't use the word "you" liberally in your website copy, you will lose a ton of business.

Here's why. We are generally selfish creatures. To me, I'm the most important guy in the world. And I would definitely expect you to think that YOU were the most important person in the world. Fair enough?

Now, couple this fact with what we discussed in Rule 5 ("someone is coming to your website with a problem,") and you begin to see the connection. When people come to your website and start reading, they have a definite subconscious "what's in it for me?" attitude. They aren't interested in much else than how your product or service can help them. And the more you use the word "you," the more you make your product or service personal to your visitor.

In other words, the general focus should be on your readers and their needs, not yours. When writing something — anything — continually ask yourself, "What's in it for the reader?"

I'm simply stunned how many businesses don't do this. Million-dollar car websites say things like, "Our advanced suspension means passengers experience a more comfortable ride."

Think about that for a second. Aren't they trying to sell the reader on the car? Or are they somehow hoping the reader goes out and finds a passenger and gives them the brochure? How about simply saying, "Our advanced suspension means you will experience a more comfortable ride"?

This seemingly small thing makes a big difference. Using the word "you" liberally when writing really makes your web copy speak to your reader and makes them feel more involved. This is never a bad thing (by the way, when I say "you," I really mean "you" and other words from the same family, like "your").

Here's an example of "non-you" web copy:

"Boil Enterprises offers a wide range of dynamic IT solutions for businesses of any size. This is because we not only specialize in every facet of the IT industry; we also strive to find revenue saving solutions tailored to our client's needs. And not only do our solutions save our clients money, they integrate with their current legacy systems, meaning there is little in the way of retraining."

Pretty boring, isn't it? And not only is it boring, it's also hard to read, and a little standoffish. Like the company is way above everyone else offering these wonderful solutions. The sad thing is, most people write like this. It's how we were taught to write in school.

Here's the same copy rewritten with a "you" focus:

"Boil Enterprises offers a wide range of IT solutions for your business. And because we specialize in every facet of the IT industry, we're able to save you considerable money because the solutions we offer will be custom-tailored to YOUR company (and work with your existing software, meaning you won't have to retrain your personnel)."

See the difference? The second example is not only friendlier and easier to read, it's also more interesting, and draws the reader in a lot more. Plus, using "you" and "your" allows the copy to directly address the reader. That's very important: I'd MUCH rather a website say they are going to save ME money instead of saying they are going to save their clients money. Personally, I couldn't care less about their other clients, I'm far more interested in what they can do for me. And trust me, we ALL think like this on a subconscious level.

How often to use the word "you"

Okay, so I'm telling you to use the words "you" and "your" liberally. But how much is liberally?

There is no definitive answer (as usual), but I will say to use them as much as you can without your web copy sounding silly (to give you an example of sounding silly, look at the Boil Enterprises example again. I contemplated sneaking in another "you" after the word "offers," but in my mind, that would have sounded a bit funny). Well, that's yours to gauge; if it sounds funny to you, change it until it doesn't.

To give you my perspective, I generally try to use "you" or "your" in at least half the sentences I write (probably more). Five to ten times a paragraph is not odd at all (the preceding two sentence example had six uses of "you" or "your"). I don't count them, nor do I try to hit any arbitrary number. I just write with a "what's in it for them" in mind.

Speaking of counting, here's something to watch out for.

Once, I was hired to write web copy by a guy who bought a web design franchise. Meaning he really wasn't a web designer himself; he just sold design services, and the franchise office would do the design. Anyway, this guy's main office gave all franchisees these silly little tools to use, and one of these tools was a simple JavaScript program that counted the word "you" in any piece of copy. And if it came back under a certain number, it would automatically say the copy wasn't customer focused enough.

Sure enough, after I sent (really good) copy to this guy, he ran it through his toy and came back to me with, "Gee Dan, it really could be more customer focused."

I answered with, "What makes you say that?"

Of course, he couldn't tell me (because he didn't know). His counter told him to tell me that. I then explained to him that the copy was already extremely customer focused (because I did use a good amount of "you," etc.), but just arbitrarily adding MORE "yous" to satisfy his dumb toy would ruin it. If I sound annoyed, it's because I was. It's not that I don't like criticism (I honestly don't mind it at all. Trust me, you get a lot of criticism as a writer, and need a thick skin). It's just that I do not like it when someone tells me that something is specifically wrong with my writing, but got his information from something as silly as a word counter. Especially someone who bought a web design franchise (which is an insult to real web designers everywhere).

Listen, don't trust stuff like this. There is no way for a program to decipher how customer focused any piece of writing is. Just write with the notion of "what's in it for them" in mind, directly address your reader by using the second person as much as possible, and you'll be fine.

One more "you" myth dispelled

I was going to put this in the Rules of English rule, but decided it fit better here.

In school, we're generally taught not to mix writing styles. A story begun in the second person remains in the second person. I say hogwash (actually, I'd use a different word, but it's a family book). You can do anything you want; my website is a mixture of first, second, and third person writing. Sometimes I talk about "I," most of the time I talk about "you," and sometimes I even get into third person and talk about "they" (or in my case, I'll say "our clients"). I'm sure I've even done it in the same sentence (you wouldn't believe how simple it is).

The bottom line is this — if it sounds good to you, use it.

Rule 9: Bolds, Italics, Underlines, Parentheses, Dashes, and Other Formatting Tricks

"Dan, there's no nice way for me to say this, but you are an extremely sloppy writer when it comes to formatting and certain pieces of punctuation. You use too many parentheses, you break form all the time, you use dashes instead of proper punctuation like colons, etc. I generally like what you write a lot, but this blatant disregard for proper structure is going to have to stop if you ever want anyone to take you seriously. Without the formatting mistakes, this paper is worth an A instead of the C you received."

— One of Dan's high school English teachers, 1982 or 1983

"Yeah, what do I know? I just write for a living.

— Dan's fantasy response

Okay, so it's 25-plus years after the fact now when I get to say my fantasy response. But my point remains: What is proper for school is not what is proper in business (or on the web). And nowhere is that more evident than in formatting.

My teacher was right, however — I was/am a terribly sloppy writer when it comes to formatting. But, in my defense, that's on purpose. Maybe it's wrong in the sense of getting an A, but I simply feel that if your writing LOOKS interesting, it will READ more interesting.

And take it from me, adding a healthy amount of formatting makes your writing that much more interesting.

Let's go over some of the things that I use (by the way, many of these are computer aided, which I didn't have in high school. I think I would have driven my teacher insane if I could have used italics and the like)!

Bolds and italics

Bolds and italics are used to put emphasis on a word or a phrase. I use these often (easily on every page, and usually in every other paragraph or so). However, don't overdo it. Too many bolds and the like will make your copy seem full of hype. Those long sales letter pages use a TON of bolds and italics, so try not to look like them.

Here's part of an example I wrote earlier:

> "We do things a little differently here at XYZ Software Development. That's because we are a true custom developer — we do not sell "out of the box" solutions. We instead focus on solving your customer service processing issues by developing software that works for **your specific situation.**"

See how I bolded that final part to add emphasis? But you can bold (or italicize) a ton of different words here to make whatever points are most important to you. Like this:

> "We do things a little differently here at XYZ Software Development. **That's because we are a true custom developer** — we do not sell "out of the box" solutions. We instead focus on solving your customer service processing issues by developing software that works for your specific situation. "

Or use both, like this:

> "We do things a little differently here at XYZ Software Development. That's because we are a true custom developer — we do not sell "out of the box" solutions. We instead focus on **solving** your customer service processing issues by developing software that works for *your specific situation.* "

They are all fine examples. You can do just about anything and it'll read well. Just DON'T do this:

> "We do things a little differently here at XYZ Software Development. That's because we are a **true custom developer** — we do *not* sell "out of the box" solutions. We **instead** focus on **solving** your customer service processing issues by *developing* software that **works** for your specific situation."

That's WAY too much, and detracts from the points that you want to emphasize.

Different color fonts

I use different color fonts (usually red or blue) every now and again when I want to make something really stand out, without beating them over the head with it. For example, on a recent client page, I wrote, "We service many Fortune 500 companies, and literally save them *millions of dollars* a year. "

I put "millions of dollars" in italics, light blue font. It stood out quite nicely, but in a tasteful, non hype-y way.

Highlighting

I stay away from highlighting for the most part. However, I admit, it REALLY makes something stand out when you use highlighting (particularly yellow). However, those hype-filled sales letter pages use highlighting a LOT, which has given it a stigma. Many people see highlighting and automatically think "hype."

So given that, I might use it once or twice in a twenty page site (and NEVER on a home page).

Underlining

Unless it's a link, stay away from underlining words on a web page. Underlining looks like a link, and when people click an underlined word and find out it's not a link, there's a brief second of disappointment. We don't want that, so don't underline anything unless it's a link.

ALL CAPS

A single word capitalized can be used sparingly in place of a bold or italic. However, when online, ALL CAPS suggests SHOUTING (they also sometimes suggest someone who cannot operate the CAPS LOCK key on his or her keyboard). So I use ALL CAPS very sparingly in web copy.

Dashes

As you must have surmised by now, I LOVE dashes. I use them all the time, and not just in the places you'd expect (like in between a phone number or in a hyphenated word, etc). I use them liberally — in fact, you could say I use them in place of commas or semicolons in many cases. I also use them to add a bit onto an end of a sentence. Generally, in my mind, a dash is a short pause, and it LOOKS good as well. I love them.

Dashes were one of the pieces of formatting I used that drove my teachers nuts. But that didn't matter to me — I liked them (the dashes, not the teachers) — so I used them. By the way, I noticed in my last book that the editor replaced all of my short "minus sign" dashes (which is the only one I use) with a much longer dash that almost touched the words it was in between — like this. That is NOT how I intended it. I like the short one a lot better. Regardless of whether it is proper or not, the long one takes away from the effect I intend. So if you see long dashes in this tome, that's the editor, not me.*

Dashes are also very effective for "asides" in your writing, when you want to make another point without breaking the sentence. For example, one could write:

"Dan Furman — who braved the dangers of Dead Man's Hill — was one of the most fearless young men in all of Pheasant Hill."

The dashes allow you to place an aside in the middle of the sentence, without losing track of the sentence's point (which is Dan's fearlessness … you know, as I re-read that, it occurs to me that the small neighborhood I grew up in — Pheasant Hill — is very mild sounding in name. It's hard to be considered tough when you're from "Pheasant Hill." Perhaps that's why we strove to make our hangout spots somewhat ominous-sounding … The Gully, The Sandpits, Dead Man's Hill, etc.)

Dashes are exceptionally useful for businesses in this sense — they lend an air of authority to your writing, while also making the writing easier to read (plus, they also help your writing sound more confident, which we already know is good).

To give another "aside" example (using yet another fictional plumbing business), one could say:

"No Leak Plumbing LLC — which has been serving Frog Lick County since 1974 — has just opened a new bath showroom at 144 Woolly Bear Lane."

In essence, the aside you create by using dashes allows you to sneak in another selling point (in this case, how long the company has been in business and where they serve), without losing the original point. It would otherwise be somewhat awkward to get in the "since 1974" part if you didn't use the aside.

---

*EDITOR'S NOTE: Sorry Dan. I, too, love all kinds of dashes, but it's my job to make sure we're using them correctly, at least where it doesn't interfere with your voice.

Again, like every other piece of formatting, this has its place, but don't overuse it. I use dashes in probably one third of the sentences I write — enough to take advantage of their good looks and ease of reading, but not enough so anyone confuses my writing with Morse code. And speaking of Morse code, here's another formatting piece I like a lot …

Ellipses …

I typically only use ellipses (three dots) to end a sentence / paragraph where I want the reader to pause and think for a second. I realize that's not the technical use for them (they are usually used in place of an omitted word or unspoken thought), but this isn't a technical book. It's also for looks — using ellipses once or twice in (say) a five page site lends an air of authority and once again shows some confidence. You can use them almost anywhere where the point you are making is clear, but you also want the reader to remember it. For example:

"SlushFund Accounting is not only thorough in regards to your deductions, we will stand behind you in the case of an IRS audit. This is what sets us apart from other accounting firms, many of whom would leave you out to dry … "

The ellipses look good, draw attention to the paragraph / statement, and also somewhat encourage the reader to make up his or her own ending.

Overdoing punctuation

Once in a great while, I'll use several pieces of punctuation instead of one (in regards to question marks or exclamation points). Saying, "And we're also the best bargain in town!" gives that sentence a little more oomph. However, like all the others, don't overdo this one — too many "!s" and "?s" and you'll sound like a lovestruck grade-schooler writing a, "Do you like me? Yes or no? Circle one" note.

And again, much of this formatting that I am discussing is not necessarily dependent upon the intended or correct use of the punctuation, but is more for looks and confidence than anything else.

Okay, one more piece of formatting, and it's my favorite.

(Parentheses)

In school, I was told over and over that I used too many of these — whatever. I just didn't care (nor did I change my style). It resulted in low grades, but like I said at the beginning of this rule, I am a successful writer (which is what I wanted to be) so I must be doing something right.

Parentheses allow you to put an aside in, a comment, and allow you to "step outside" of what you are saying, without breaking the thought. They are pretty self explanatory — the preceding paragraph has two great examples of using parentheses to make an aside/comment. In my mind, they are almost interchangeable with dashes, except sometimes parentheses are a little better at inserting humor or a comment in the middle of a sentence. A dash aside just seems somewhat more serious, while parentheses can be either serious or a bit goofy.

The bigger question here is why are asides so important? Let's answer it.

Why asides are important

I could never be an actor, because I'd be tempted to break the fourth wall way too much. But in writing, you can break the fourth wall, and, in my opinion, it usually enhances what you are doing / saying. Especially in a business sense, and even more so online.

We already talked about writing like you talk, the importance of being interesting, bringing your reader along with you, and writing with confidence — well, using asides is an excellent and effective way to do all four of these things. Asides (whether in parentheses or dashes) basically say to the reader, "Hey, I'm like you — we're buddies. I'll tell you all this good stuff, but every now and again, I'll whisper a comment in your ear that only you can hear."

That's the effect asides have — it's almost like you are speaking directly to the one person reading (even if there are 1,000 singular people reading). It makes the reader feel a little special, and it also shows a LOT of confidence — it's the writer who is sure of himself or herself that dares to break form.

In closing

Start using these formatting pieces in your writing. Use a bold here and there — throw in an italic somewhere. Use a dash (or three) somewhere, and see how it looks to you. Use an aside — either a joke or something serious — and read it back to yourself … does it make the writing more interesting? I'll bet almost anything it does.

Rule 10: Lots of Escape Hatches (Calls to Action)

This is a really short rule, but it's a pretty important one for web copy. You need to give your reader the opportunity to contact you (or buy) on a consistent basis. And you need to not only give them the opportunity, but most times, you need to blatantly ASK for action.

Success in sales ultimately depends on asking for the order. All good (and even lousy) salespeople know that. You can have the best sales presentation imaginable, but if you don't ASK for the order, you won't make the sale. And it's the same with websites and web copy. You can have the best website in the world, but it won't help you one bit if you do not ask people to buy or contact you. And I mean repeatedly.

SAMPLE 13
NUMEROUS CALLS TO ACTION

There are two ways to do this, and you should use both:

1. Put a direct link to your Quote (or Buy) page in your navigation bar. This way, no matter what page a visitor is visiting on your site, doing business with you is a click away, in a predictable place.

2. Put numerous links to contact you in your copy. I usually find the paragraph summary (or last line in a paragraph) works well. You need not have it say, "Click here to contact us" either — more and more, good SEO means you should have keywords in links (and currently, links are weighted more heavily than regular text) — so perhaps having a link with some keywords works well. Sample 13 is an example using the template.

I'm touting some features and benefits, and then basically giving the reader a choice: Contact me now, or read on. This works very well. And it also gets in keywords and keyphrases.

Now I'll admit that this example could be a little overkill for some sites (it's a little hype-y to do it after every paragraph), but certainly any site, no matter how "upscale," could comfortably do the second one.

There are two reasons for giving the reader so many escape hatches (essentially meaning calls to action.) Clever term, isn't it? The first is obvious — you tell some benefits, then you essentially say, "Heard enough? Well, here's how you get one!"

The second reason is for most sites, the navigation bar will eventually scroll off the screen. Well, we don't want anyone to have to go look for it, do we? Let's give everyone an easy way to contact you at any moment, no matter where they are on the page. Do NOT underestimate how important this is. I have had clients tell me, "Oh, if they want to contact me, they'll scroll back up."

I have news for them: No, many people won't. It's little stuff like this that separates the successful sites from the ones that do nothing. I've proven it over and over.

There, that's simple, isn't it? Lots of escape hatches.

One more rule, and I can finally put this chapter to bed.

Rule 11: Be an Oreo®

This was going to be a nice, easy 10-rules chapter. But the more I thought about it, there was something else I wanted to say, and I couldn't figure out where else it would fit in this book. So I made an 11th rule.

Rule 11 is not really a rule of writing, per se. But it is something you should always be thinking about when you write for your website.

And that rule is to be an Oreo® … Okay, let me explain what this ultra-clever (or ultra-corny — I can't decide) metaphor means.

What do I mean by "be an Oreo®?"

One of my favorite snacks is that old American standby of cookies and milk. I like all kinds of cookies: chocolate chip, peanut butter, graham crackers, etc. But my favorite is the Oreo. Not Double Stuf or chocolate ones, but the plain old classic Oreo. Six Oreos and a glass of milk is an awesome dessert.

When I was young, we didn't have a lot of money, so my mom cut corners where she could. And one of the things that were cut were name brands. Coke became "store brand cola," Bounty became "Money Saving Brand Paper Towels," etc. And it affected my beloved Oreos, too. Oreos became "store brand cream-filled cookies."

And my mom's mantra of "they're just as good" (usually code for "it's crap") was used again and again.

Well, in some Bizarro-world, maybe some "off-brand" things truly are "just as good." But the store brand cookies my mom bought weren't one of them. A poor imitation of Oreos they were. In fact, there are several brands, some of them even name brands, that try to copy an Oreo, and none of them can do it; they just aren't the same. Trust me, I know Oreos.

Bottom line, if you want an Oreo, then you have to buy Oreos. Period. Nothing else can be an Oreo but an Oreo.

Thus, I want you to think in terms of being an Oreo in your particular field.

See, in my business, there must be thousands of "writing" websites. Most of them are awful, a scant few are decent, and even a scanter few are good. But, in my mind, out of these thousands of sites out there, I stand alone.

Why do I stand alone? Because nobody out there writes like ME, and I make that very evident in my website's copy. If you want "a writer," you can hire one of a hundred people. But if you want ME, well, you have to hire ME. There is no substitute.

My website is very clear that I am not only a professional writer, but within my web copy I go over — in detail — the nuances of my writing style and the like. It's evident not only in what I say, but how I say it. My website has tons of personality. Most of my competition doesn't do this — they say, "Hey, we're writers, here are a few things we do, click here to hire us."

There's no pizzazz, no personality, and nothing special on their sites that sets them apart.

The result is I get people that want to hire ME, as opposed to hiring any old writer. Which is good, because that cuts out all the competition; try as they may, but nobody can compete with me at being me. I like to say I compete with all writers, while also competing with nobody. I do not have the lowest price or the fastest service, but I am the best at being Dan Furman, at any price. Thus, I make damn sure that the "Dan Furman writing style" aspect is touted on my website. If people want Dan Furman, they can't hire Chuckles McNoodle and expect the same results. They have to hire ME.

So when you are writing your site and working the first ten rules in (and everything else I have taught you so far), keep in mind what it is that makes you special as a business. What you do better than anyone else out there? Mention it on your site. Tout it. Write a paragraph somewhere that says why you do this one particular thing better than anyone. Then, like I showed you, sum that paragraph up with a bold statement that touts your specialty.

Now, the special aspect of yours could be quite small. It need not be like mine. Maybe you have lower overhead and a better price. Maybe your product is better quality, maybe your company services clients within one hour, maybe you're "the singing accountant." The list is endless, and I'm confident that there's something that your company does that nobody else can do/provide/claim. And this "thing," whatever it is, should make it onto your website somewhere. This can also be considered part of niche marketing, which I discuss at length in *Start and Run a Real Home-Based Business,* another title published by Self-Counsel Press.

A Clever Example of "Oreoism"

Growing up, there was this one road we'd drive every so often to go into New Jersey. And on the way home, I always recall seeing this one billboard for a local liquor store. The billboard said something like, "We're the last liquor store before the ski areas," meaning if you wanted a bottle of Bourbon for your ski weekend, well, this was your last shot.

Now, this wouldn't be remarkable enough to put into a book except for the fact that this liquor store bordered the freaking ski areas. Of course it was the last one; there was literally no room between it and the road that entered the ski area. You couldn't put a liquor store closer to the ski area if you wanted to.

So here they took a mundane, obvious fact, and turned themselves into the Oreo of liquor stores before the ski area.

Neat, huh?

In your town / city, you have local competition. In your state, you have statewide competition. In your country, you have country-wide competition. But online, you generally compete with the entire world. So it's to your advantage to have a website that has a little personality, a little something that says "NOBODY can do what we do, and that's because … "

Yes, you will always have competition. So make a small part of yourself that nobody else can compete with.

Be an Oreo online. It works wonders.

INTERMISSION

It's time for a little intermission.

The reason for this is simple: I have a few things I want to reiterate and/or go over, and they don't fit into any other chapters. They are similar to the "how this book works" part of the introduction, but you've already read that, and I doubt you want to go backwards.

Plus, lots of cool things have an intermission. Broadway plays, the opera, and highbrow concerts have an intermission. Epic movies have an intermission. *Monty Python and the Holy Grail* had an intermission. And even Pink Floyd had an intermission when I saw them in the late '80s (I was at one of the Nassau Coliseum shows that spawned the live record and video. If you look really hard on the "Delicate Sound of Thunder" video, you can see me. I'm the one in the Pink Floyd t-shirt waving and cheering).

So since all things with an intermission are decidedly cool (even opera), I decided my book should have an intermission as well.

Short Recap

Even though we've only been through four official chapters, we're well over halfway done here (indeed, right now, I'm at about 42,000 words, and I planned for the entire book to be in the mid 50s, so this is definitely a late intermission). This book was originally conceived as a website writing book, but what I had to say on just website writing took about 25,000 words; not enough for a real book (I really don't pad my books with fluff. I give good info, and then I move on). I also wanted to write a book on website setup and structure; again, that was maybe 30,000 words, not enough for a real book. So combining the two (which makes a ton of sense) works very well.

So far, we've gone over why things like targeted traffic matters, what a good website needs, basic website setup, and things like that. Basic website setup then led into writing, and the writing chapter was easily the longest chapter in this book (the rest of the book will seem positively brief by comparison). In fact, it's the longest chapter I ever wrote in any work. And I'm proud of it; as I re-read it, I am satisfied that it is an exceptional primer on writing for business. Which is why I wanted this intermission: I want to reiterate how to use the information I have just spent 40,000-plus words giving you.

The website setup parts are pretty self explanatory. The basic points I am looking to drive home are to know where your traffic is coming from, understand what your visitors are looking for, and then deliver it to them in an easy-to-read, uncluttered fashion. None of the points I make are set in stone; you are free to experiment to your heart's content. And you may very well find something that works a little better, too (if so, let me know and I'll try to work you into the next book).

Heck, *I* learn new stuff every day. It's part of what makes this so interesting.

I reiterate this because we have slowly become a society that wants things done for us 100%. We don't want a book that teaches us concepts, we want to be held by the hand and be given a "business in a box," where all we have to do is buy it, turn it on, and collect money.

That's not the way things work, which is why I'm such a big advocate of testing. Test EVERYTHING. Test headlines, test page order, test subheadings, test calls to action, test it all. If you don't test (and tweak) on a consistent basis, you will lose online business. It's that simple. There is no "business in a box" or "foolproof system." There are logical, sound business concepts (which is what I am teaching you), and there is testing.

If you run the business and website yourself, this may mean doing a little dirty work (well, as dirty as online work can be. In my experience, except for some dust that gathers around the computer, it's pretty spiffy). You'll have to learn how to get your website statistics, and then how to analyze them (for the record, I use a program called "Web Log Storming," and I've included a link to this from the web resources page on the CD).

Even if you are the big boss (with underlings to manipulate), it still might mean looking at the website statistics and making a decision based on what you see. What I'm trying to say is that there is no magic bullet. The suggestions I give you work very well for me and my clients, and have been honed and proven over the years. I want you to take the suggestions I am giving and work them into YOUR situation, not the other way around. And there is always room for improvement and evolvement. Do not rest on your laurels.

It's the same for the writing. I'm not trying to teach you to write "just like me." That would be impossible. Just like you couldn't teach me to write like you do. We all write the way we write, and no book is going to change that to any large degree. However, I STRONGLY feel that I can make you a better writer (especially a better website copywriter and general business writer) by just showing you a few rules that you can then work into your own particular style. For example, by just inserting a few confidence statements and words into your writing, along with a few one-sentence paragraphs, can drastically change the tone (and effectiveness) of the piece, whether it's online or for a résumé cover letter. Just adding a bulleted link list to your home page can triple conversions overnight — I've seen it happen time and time again.

Take that chapter on writing and really dive into it. Mark it up with a highlighter, refer to it when you are writing something, etc. You need not use everything in there; like I said, even just one or two of the rules can really help your website convert better, which is the entire point of this book.

Moving Forward

The rest of the book is going to fly by. This is because I've already mentioned the most salient points regarding websites, webpages, and writing. Now all I need to do is briefly go over what the individual pages need, get into a few things regarding SEO, show you a few more tricks in regards to landing pages and small microsites, and then wrap things up.

Next up are three chapters that talk about individual pages. Fair warning, they will be fairly short chapters. Also, instead of endlessly referring back to the rules, I am going to include the "three most important rules" for most of them. This doesn't mean they are the only three that matter for that page, but they are the ones that I feel warrant the most attention. It goes without saying that ALL rules should be at least thought about for every page (hmmm … I guess since I said it, it doesn't go without saying anymore …)

Okay, I hope you've enjoyed this tome so far. Let's go learn some more.

5

WRITING FOR YOUR HOME PAGE

Most important rules to remember when writing for your home page:

- 🖙 Rule 1 (scan-able copy)
- 🖙 Rule 5 (do not preach to the choir)
- 🖙 Rule 8 (use the word "you" a lot)

By a wide margin, your home page is the most important page of your website. It welcomes visitors, it lets them know they can get what they came for, and it sets the tone for your entire site. A bad home page can completely kill your website and your online presence. A good home page can invite people in and encourage them to learn more about you.

If you spend any time at all online, you'll see hundreds of examples of home pages. And to be honest, most of them are pretty bad. It would appear that many cater to the ego of the web designer and/or wish to show off some technical pizzazz. How else can one explain the myriad of websites that open with some silly Flash movie or similar? Putting a tiny "skip intro" button doesn't help, either — time and time again, I've seen website statistics overwhelmingly suggest that people leave when they see a website open with a movie.

The Three Main Things the Writing on Your Home Page Needs to Address

1. **Welcome your visitor by addressing the reason they came:** As I've already mentioned numerous times, your visitors largely came to your site for a reason. ADDRESS THAT REASON in a clear, uncluttered fashion that speaks directly to the visitor. Let your visitor know that you can solve the problem he or she came to solve. And don't try to sell him or her on the merits of your industry — instead, sell the merits of YOU. Mention what you can do for your visitor (save millions of dollars, increase sales, ensure house is always clean, etc.).

2. **Give clear choices on what you offer:** Make it easy for your visitor to find what he or she is looking for. Not only should you have a navigation bar somewhere, but having links right in your copy helps as well — this allows someone to read a bit and jump off when he or she sees something he or she likes. Subheadings and bullet points work very well in this regard.

    Now, we have to take a moment here and understand that while I like giving people choices in where to go next, I do NOT advocate having a bunch of different info/link boxes (etc.) scattered throughout the page. Things should be orderly, not scattershot. You don't need a link column on your left, boxes on the bottom, a box on the right for latest news, and three services links underneath that — someone will look at that and not know where to click next — it's just not orderly.

    Having links from within the copy is okay (and even encouraged). Having a sidebar with a little information and a button/link is okay. But having three or four separate areas on your home page isn't okay. The main text should be clear, and the side stuff should clearly be side stuff.

3. **Make sure your home page copy gives an overall picture of your business**: While doing the preceding two things, know that your home page is also an overall picture of your business. Your most important points go here. If a huge selling point of your company is that you've been around 45 years, then yes, this needs to find its way onto your home page.

Tips on Layout

Quick disclaimer: I'm not a layout guy. However, that said, I do know what makes (or breaks) a page in a design sense.

In essence, the design should NOT get in the way of anything, and should offer an inviting canvas for the words. For most businesses, too much "stuff" doesn't work. Overly clever design doesn't work.

There are probably four million examples I can give of "bad" things to do on a home page in regards to design. In fact, they can (and have) filled entire books. So instead, I am going to give you two examples of how to do it right in regards to design / layout / writing.

Now, I have to admit, I am quite boring in my theory on web design. I like simple. I like a nice, square canvas for the main body text. I like defined navigation. I'm not opposed to a second section for words, but I do not want it to get in the way of what I have to offer. I also like white (or very light) backgrounds (no picture backgrounds, please) and dark (usually black) text. Yes, it's boring, but boring does good online business.

Okay, here's the first example. You've seen this picture before — it's the home page on my main site.

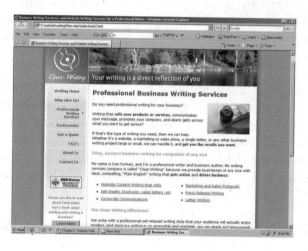

Let's take a look at what I have going on here. To start, I have my logo on the top left — so you know where you landed. I have a nice picture with a slogan. I then have a "writing" picture on the right, and a nice headline that clearly shows what I offer. Great start.

If you want to scan this page, you can. Through use of bolds, bullets, and sub-headings, you'll scan and come away with the following snippets: professional writing services; sell your products; get you results; drives business; business writing for companies of any size ... then a few links to specific services. Oh, and we're different, too.

All that, in a two second glance. If you were looking for a site that offers writing that makes you money, my website largely delivered.

There are also clear links on the left, I get my Better Business Bureau plug in, you can easily go get a quote ... there's really a lot going on here.

Plus, most people see all of this without scrolling (depends on monitor size, but most people now have at least a 17-inch). Then, if you scroll just a teeny bit, I get into my Oreo spiel — how I'm different, etc.

I do not want you to think I am tooting my own horn here or trolling for business (truth be told, I'm expensive. Fair warning to those who wish to use my services). I merely want to show you the best example of what I am teaching. I also want to clearly show you that I indeed practice the things I preach. Now, obviously, I do not use every rule that I've mentioned in this page. There's no paragraph summary (that you can see, anyway), there's no confidence statement, etc. You just can't do everything everywhere. But I do utilize the most important things: It's scan-able, I solve a visitor's problem (and don't preach to the choir), and I engage the reader by using "you" a lot.

This page works very, very well for me. I get a ton of action out of it. Some people read the whole thing, others contact me right away, and still others peruse the links and move deeper into the site.

Success Is Small

Here's the kicker of this success. Most people who see my site move on right away, never to contact me or read another word of mine. That's the reality of the web: Success is measured in very small numbers. If I can get 10 people out of 100 to take notice of something, man, I succeeded BIG TIME. Always remember that success online is a much smaller number than you want to think it is.

Okay, there's a second example, in Sample 14. This is the site I made for my first book.

This site is a little different in that it is for one thing only: my book. Thus, I can be a little more tightly focused. Basically, I'm looking for someone to be interested enough to go to Amazon (or wherever) and order it. But again, a lot of the rules and techniques I preach are present —

- I address the reason people came,

- I make it scan-able,

- I talk directly to the reader, and

- I make it simple to figure out where to go next.

Now because this site is for the book, and the book alone, I can get away with a little sidebar on the right where I kind of joke around. In fact, the book is somewhat marketed as a funny book, so having that little sidebar helps. I'm not selling to a myriad of situations on this site, I'm just selling my book. (On my main writing site,

TIGHTER FOCUS HOME PAGE EXAMPLE

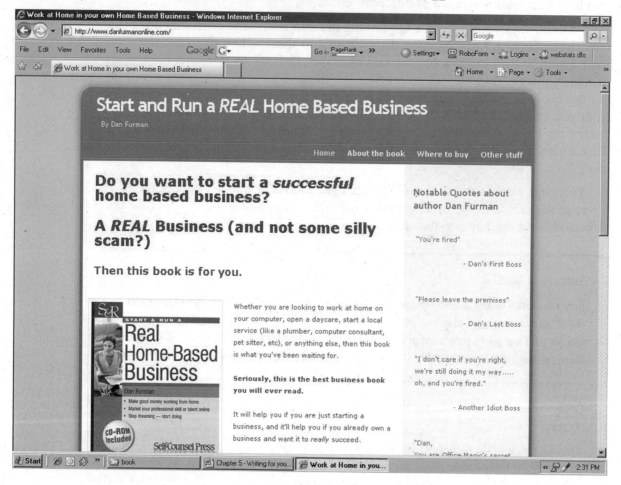

I get everyone from website owners needing copy to Fortune 500 companies needing a proposal, to people looking for a letter to keep them out of jail. I need to address all of these types of situations. My book site doesn't need to be so wide in focus.)

Again, I get good play on this site. It does exactly what I want it to do (tells people about my book and drives them to purchase it).

Notice on these two sites that neither is cluttered with "stuff" — they are fairly simple to understand and navigate. Yes, the writing website has a little more going on, but it's a much bigger focus. But even though there's a lot happening, there's really no confusion over what to do next or such — if you need writing, I probably have a link that will interest you, and I make that plain as day (but again, only a scant few follow through, and that's perfectly okay).

Also, the book website is an example of what is called a microsite. I'll go over microsites more in Chapter 10.

Now look at Sample 15, a page that didn't work. I'm a little embarrassed to put this here, but since I'm showing you my sites that work, it's only fair to show you one that bombed.

Now this site was fine in a design sense (really nice, in fact — my designer and I brainstormed in coming up with the chess motif, and I still like it to this day). So as far as general looks, this site does the job very nicely. If I had to nitpick, perhaps I'd make the links up top bigger and the picture a bit smaller, but that's it.

However, the biggest problems with this site are problems with MY writing and such. Here are my mistakes:

1. The sidebar stuff is distracting. VERY much so. It's not an obvious sidebar like my main writing site or my book site — this one is in your face, competing for your eye. And really, who gives a @#$% about what's new? It's not like I'm a community site where I have tons of repeat visitors — A What's New section on a site like mine is almost pretentious. If I really feel the need to tell people what's new, I can do it on the About Us page. This sidebar would not be so bad if it were a defined sidebar and less in your face. But it isn't, and it cost me.

2. The headline sucks. Plain and simple. It's just not interesting.

3. The opening line … just awful. What was I thinking? I'm not solving anyone's problem. Really, you'd be hard pressed to read further into this site.

4. The copy just doesn't "look" good. Too blocky, not enough white space. Paragraphs are too long.

5. Expanding on the last point — you can't scan this. Kiss of death.

6. Again, it's just not interesting — someone came here to find a writer, and I'm preaching to the choir, telling them how costly bad writing is (in a fairly smarmy tone, as well). Duh — I'm almost insulting my reader!

7. And what the heck is up with that thought balloon/exclamation point thing?

Net results for this site: In over 2,700 unique visits, not one contact. NOT ONE. That's abysmally bad. Plus, out of those 2,700 visitors, only maybe 100 ventured beyond the home page. Yikes.

But you know, I figured out why. And listed the reasons for you to see. Even pros sometimes write bombs — it does happen. That's why we test stuff.

Happily, my regular writing site was keeping me so busy that I abandoned the corporate writing site (this was back in 2005. I keep the site on my hard drive as a

EASILY THE WORST HOME PAGE COPY I EVER WROTE

reminder of bad concepts). But I learned painful lessons from it (actually, they weren't so painful, because it reiterated to me the concepts I already knew about what really worked and what didn't). Now trust me — the site came out exactly like I planned it — I wanted to try a smarmy, anti-corporate writing site that was different from what I was currently using. Well, that's what I got, and man, did it bomb.

Now that you've read this far into this book, can you clearly see why that site failed so miserably? I truly hope you can.

Oh, note the time again in the screenshot. It's 12:34 a.m. this time. You know what that means, don't you? It means Dan really cares (aw).

Keywords and Keyphrases

Let's talk about keywords and keyphrases a little, because these are a pretty big deal to a lot of people. In fact, people make a MUCH bigger deal out of them than they should.

Let me get something perfectly clear with you: Keywords in your web copy, in and of themselves, are really a pretty small part of the SEO process. Think about this logically: Any eight-year-old can place a ton of keywords on a page. Trust me, the search engines know this, too. Far less weight is given to keywords than you think.

I feel the need to mention this because for some reason, people seem to think that all they need are keywords on their pages to shoot up in search engine rankings. That's so far from the truth that it boggles the mind. Again, we truly learned the key-word thing in fourth grade. It was called "use the word _____ in a sentence."

Now, I'll admit that when you search for something, from within the results, the keywords are highlighted / bolded. Maybe that's why people think they are so vital? I don't know. Yes, they are important, but they don't carry nearly as much weight as the average person wants to think.

Okay, here's how you handle keywords on your home page (and all other pages). Just keep in mind what you do, and what people will be searching for, and use those terms naturally. For me, it's things like "Business Writing," "Professional Writing," "Website Writing," etc. For you, it might be "Anytown Plumber" (them again) or the like. Just use these words and phrases naturally within your text, as the anchor text in your links, and within your subheadings, and you'll be fine. Do NOT overdo it, as it sounds awful when you say, "Buy New York Mealworms from Mealworm Man of NY, who has the best NY Mealworms in New York for fishing in NY with New York Mealworms."

Yes, I'm somewhat kidding, but a lot of sites actually do say similar things to what I just wrote — don't be one of them. Besides, search engines have gotten smarter and smarter. They know when you put "mealworm" (or similar) on your page 500 times, and will certainly penalize you.

There are way more important factors in regards to SEO than keywords. It is not worth it — not for one second — to make your web copy sound silly just to get a few extra keywords or keyphrases in. I've seen sites with just a few keywords (just natu-rally within their text) get very high rankings because they do the other SEO stuff (and the search engines' algorithms change all the time).

Please commit the following phrase to memory: The site with the most keywords does NOT win.

Wrapping Up the Home Page

That was easy, wasn't it? Since I already gave you the basics earlier, and the rules of web copy, you probably could have done this on your own without this chapter. But I felt this tied it up nicely; make sure your home page is clean, easy-to-read and navigate; addresses the reason people came; and gets across the most important points.

That's really all you need to do. No real trick to it.

Again, in regards to layout and design, this really isn't the place to get all fancy. Easy, clear navigation; big square of white space for your text; dark text (main text black or dark grey is usually best, although you can use anything that is easy to read, like I did on the sidebar of the book site). Augment your text with other colors for subheadings and the like. Yes, it's not flashy, but let me tell you from years of experience that it works.

Oh wait — one more thing before we go.

I'm going to move forward to other pages in a second, but there's something else I need to tell you: Your website needs to be predictable (meaning you should keep the same basic layout throughout your entire website).

This means you really should not have a design for the home page, and then a completely different design elsewhere. If someone leaves the home page and is greeted by a completely different design, well, that's jarring. Why would anyone want to do that to a visitor? You can make small changes if needed (for example, if you have a right-hand sidebar on the home page for something, but don't need it on the other pages, it's okay to remove it — that's not too big a change. But don't go from one color scheme to another, and don't change navigation).

Okay, home page is done. Let's move onto the About Us/Why Use Us and Products/Services pages.

6
WRITING FOR YOUR ABOUT US/ WHY USE US PAGE AND YOUR PRODUCTS/SERVICES PAGES

Most important rules for your About Us/Why Use Us and Products/Services Pages:

- ✏ Rule 1 (the subheadings and bullets more than anything)
- ✏ Rule 7 (write with confidence)
- ✏ Rule 10 (lots of escape hatches)

Next up are the About Us/Why Use Us page and the Products/Services pages. I'm combining these into one chapter because they are both fairly simple in that if you read the book up to this point, you already know everything you need to know. I'll just give you a little guidance here.

Let's start with the Why Use Us (or About Us) page.

Your About Us/Why Use Us Page

Like I mentioned way back in the beginning, you can do this one of two ways: You can have an about us that sells the reader on the merits of using you, and then gets into your company history, etc., or you can have a Why Us? (why use us, why buy from us) page, and then a more traditional About Us somewhere else.

I've done it both ways, and I do think the "why" method works a little better for service-type businesses where you really feel you want to tout the reasons to do business with you. This way is very direct (the reader is clicking on the page to find out why they should hire you, and they are expecting reasons for such). This is a big deal in reader mindset (and like I have mentioned several times, it's these little things that turn readers into contacts). So if cornered, I'll recommend the "why" route. Let's go over both ways.

Straight about us page

Many larger, more professional companies feel the "why" route is a little too "salesy" (which it really isn't, but they are entitled to their opinion), so they opt for just an About Us. If you wish to go with just an About Us page, I suggest breaking it up into two (or more) parts (led off by a subheading for each).

The reason for this is simple: I strongly suggest that if you are just using an About Us page that the beginning of this page still be reasons to do business with you. This is the place to tout what makes you different, your company philosophy, how you treat customers, and how you get things done. Then you can have a second section for company history.

You're probably tired of seeing my site, so I've pasted copy I once wrote for my own About Us page into the Sample 16 template.

Okay, let's analyze this a bit. I essentially use my subheadings to break this up. I lay out the company structure and philosophy, but I do such in a way that clearly benefits the reader. I confidently take a shot at other companies (and it's so true — very few companies actually finish projects, or handle the little things — how many blogs do you see that have the last entry from four months ago? There's no easier way to say, "We don't finish stuff" than to do that). Then I provide a "contact us" link.

And after that, I tell the company story, which is pretty self explanatory. I'll provide another contact link after that story (which ends the page).

Now, if I were a larger company, I could extend this page some and have company officers, pictures of locations, or just have a link to separate pages for those things — either way works, but since I prefer shorter pages, I'd probably go with the link.

The goal here is to remember that even on your About Us page, it's not REALLY about you. It's about your reader, THEIR needs, and how you can fill them.

This is a good page to use as a stand-alone About Us page. But even though I am selling on this page, I would still rather have a Why page in addition to this About Us (and that's how I am currently doing it). This is because a Why page REALLY allows you to sell.

SAMPLE 16
ABOUT US EXAMPLE

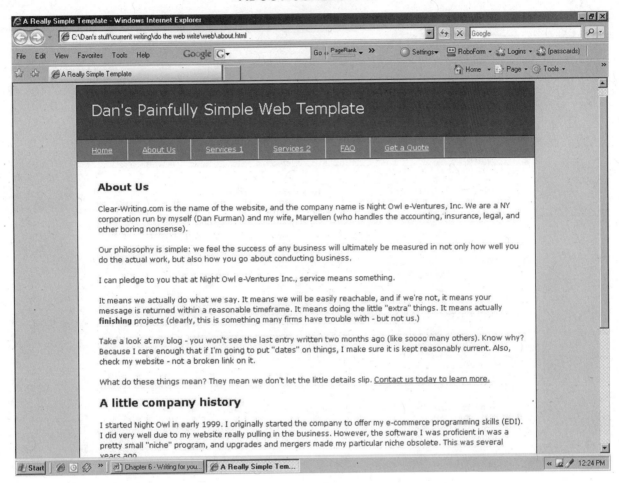

Using a why page also

Now, the page I just showed you is a pretty nice About Us page (and it's what I am using now), but I do like using both an About Us and a Why Us page. The Why Us page allows you to sell just a little harder. If you try to sell HARD on your About Us, well, it just doesn't work. The About Us that I just showed you is a good example of the soft sell. But here's an example of what you can do with a Why page (again, pasted into Sample 17).

Let's look at this now — I'm not really saying the same things that I am on my About Us page, am I? Instead, I'm really hammering what makes my writing different. Yes, I could have done this on the beginning of the About Us page, but it would really seem a little out of place (in my mind anyway).

WHY USE US EXAMPLE

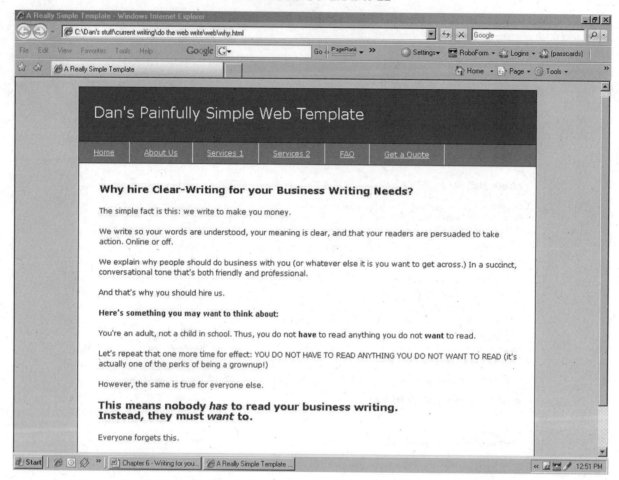

This is why I like to use both. And it's what I suggest. Use a Why Us-type page for your second page, and then later in the site, use an About Us page.

That's about all I have to say about the Why Us and About Us pages. Let's move onward to the Products/Services pages.

Products / Services Pages

Another really short thing to note, because you already know what you need to know. The same three rules are the most important for Products/Services pages (1, 7, and 10). Let's do Services first, because they are popular.

Services page(s)

The main thing you need to decide is to have one Services page, or one page for each service you offer. This will depend on your business, but I find that the more you can break up your services, the better off you are. This allows you to really specialize on niches, allows you to possibly use more than one landing page (more on that in Chapter 9), is better for SEO purposes, and makes you seem more specialized.

Even if you are, say, an accountant, you can break your services up into several chunks, depending on where your specialties lay. For example, you could have "Small Business Accounting," "Restaurant Accounting," "Professional Trades Accounting," etc. Use the flyout method I described in Chapter 3 and have a page for each.

Now, what to write on these pages? Just go through the rules and use what I have taught you. Again, here's an example (you've seen this picture already, but it's worth placing again — it's my website writing page, one of my main Services pages).

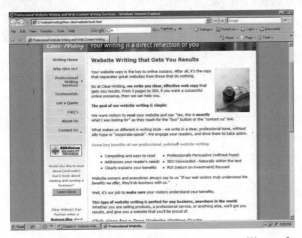

If you can make out the very bottom of the copy, you'll see from the tops of the words that I have a link in huge letters ("Click Here for a Website Writing Quote"). So I'm offering an escape hatch in addition to everything that's going on here.

Now this is a pretty big and elaborate Services page, because I am using it as a landing page as well (again, more on that in Chapter 9). You don't have to be this elaborate. You can just have a subheading, a few confident paragraphs, and then a link to contact you. Like this press release page (which isn't a landing page).

SAMPLE 18
SHORT SERVICES PAGE EXAMPLE

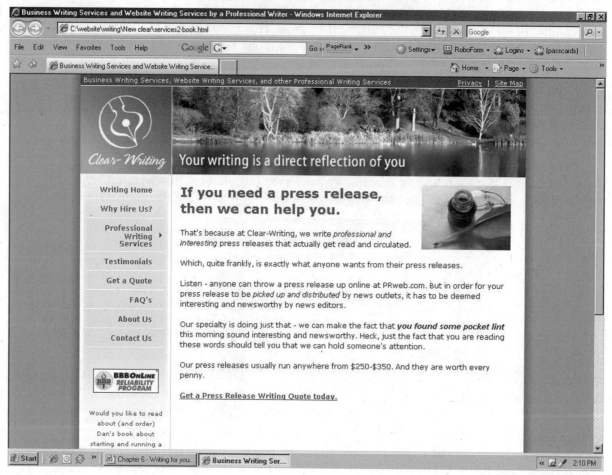

I just talk a bit about the press releases, tout why mine are better, make a small joke about the pocket lint, and ask them to contact me. Simple, really (and it works really nice).

One more picture (again, this is a repeat — it's the anchor text picture, but it shows a great example of putting several small services on one page).

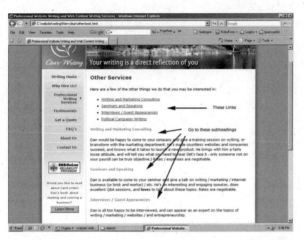

If you really wanted to, you could put a contact link after each service. I opted not to since the page is pretty short and I have one in the navigation bar, and another on the page bottom (which you can't see here).

That's it on Services pages — long, short, it doesn't matter. Do it however you think it best suits you (and, err, test the results).

Products pages

This is the easiest part of the book for me. The exact same things I just went over in services apply to products also. Save for one: Have a "buy" link after every product.

If your product needs a lot of room, give it its own page. If it doesn't need that much room, put a few on a page. Just like services. There, that was simple.

Quick Tip: How Far to Branch Out?

Some companies have a large array of branches in regards to products and/or services. What I mean is this:

The one SERVICES link on the navigation bar branches into ACCOUNTING SERVICES and IT SERVICES, which each of those then branching into several more services (like IT might branch into ERP and WEB SERVICES).

In general terms, I do NOT recommend this "Russian Doll" approach. That's because it starts to get tiresome and confusing. Let's keep it on one level. If you must, put TWO services top pages on the Navigation bar (IT and Accounting in this case), and then have those branch out one level each.

Frequently Asked Questions (and Answers)

Q: Okay, why do you like this whole FAQ thing, Dan?

A: There are really several good reasons. First, an FAQ does the obvious — it answers those frequent questions (cutting down on email questions, which saves you time). Second, it lets you get across great selling points, because you can lob yourself softball questions and then knock them out of the park. Third, it allows you to get in a ton of keywords and keyphrases. Last, it un-clutters other areas of your website by giving you a place to get across all those things you want to get across, but don't fit elsewhere.

Q: I get the "frequent questions" part to cut down on email (that's obvious, after all), but can you explain the others more? For example, how does an FAQ let you get across great selling points by lobbing softball questions?

A: I just demonstrated that with this question. Let me explain further: I wanted to get across the point of lobbing softball questions. So I asked myself it here in this book, and am answering now. It's akin to talking to yourself, but in a Q&A form. You can do this with anything — ask yourself the question, "Can you Explain Your

Rate Structure?" then answer it (and, of course, show what a value you are). You can do this with anything … say you offer free shipping on certain orders. You can ask the FAQ question, "How do I qualify for free shipping?" Just make a list of the main points you really want to reiterate and sell, and make up FAQ questions about them.

You can then draw the reader in further by making the FAQ almost a conversation for a question or two (like I am doing here).

Q: How does an FAQ section let you add in keywords and keyphrases?

A: Well, take my business for example. I can ask the FAQ question, "What are your rates for web copy?" and then answer it by saying, "Rates for web copy (which is sometimes referred to as website writing, website copy, web copywriting, and/or a myriad of other names) often depend on the complexity of … " etc. I can get away with adding all of these in the FAQ because, unlike other pages, your FAQ can be very informal and freeform, and is not really a selling page (for example, you read earlier how I couldn't really do that exact same thing on my website writing page).

You see, I realize that readers are fairly "deep" into my site (for lack of a better word) once they hit the FAQ. So at this point in my website, I'm not as concerned with holding them as I am in making a point and marketing. I've already held them, as evidenced just by them being at the FAQ in the first place.

Q: How about de-cluttering other areas? Expand on that.

A: Well, on my website, I want to talk about my rates at some point. I want to talk about my work process. I want to mention that I'm usually fairly busy, and typically not available tomorrow (you'd be surprised at how many people think I'm sitting here with nothing to do). These things tend to clutter up other pages and get in the way of my selling message, but they work GREAT in an FAQ section.

So the FAQ becomes a catch-all place for these pieces of information that I want to talk about, but can't seem to fit in anywhere else.

Q: Should I ask (and then answer) questions like "Why are your rates so low?" or "Why are you such a good value?" Those seem like good softballs.

A: NO. There's a difference between softball and T-ball. Those are really … unprofessional. Instead, make the question say, "Can you expand on your fee structure?" or similar.

The "why are your rates so low?" question (or similar) is such an obvious fluff question that it's almost a turnoff.

Q: What questions should I be asking?

A: There are a lot of things you should be discussing in your FAQ. Here are a few ideas to spur your creative juices:

- Your rates / fees / prices (but again, in a classy way, not a "why are you so cheap?" way).

- Your work process (how thorough you are, how much you care about clients, how you finish what you start).

- What separates you from others (and yeah, this one you can ask just like that, i.e., "What separates you from your competition?")

- Your hours/days/weeks of operation.

- Your scheduling and similar (like I mentioned, I want to let people know that I'm really not a "rush job" guy, so I do so in my FAQ).

- What you will and won't do.

- Deposit requirements / how you accept payment (credit cards, billing terms, etc.)

- The areas you service (and this is a great way to get city, town, and county keyphrases in. For example, in answering the question, "What areas do you service?," you could answer with, "We handle plumbing in Anytown, plumbing in Another Town, plumbing in Small Town, and even plumbing in Big Town." Again, we're answering the question, but we're doing it differently than I've advocated everywhere else. The FAQ is the one place where you can get a little silly with keyphrases without it sounding bad or hurting you.)

- Any other little thing you can think of. For example, I answer questions regarding whether I do edits for things already written (yes, I do); if I need to be an expert in an industry before I write about it (no); who owns the writing when I'm finished (the client does); and whether I do graphic design (no. And trust me, you wouldn't want me to).

Q: So it sounds like you are somewhat ignoring some of the rules and such. Like the keywords thing you just mentioned.

A: Yes, that is correct. The FAQ is the one area where you can go a little nuts with keywords, keyphrases, etc.

Q: Is being informal in a FAQ (like you are here) okay?

A: Absolutely! I'm a big fan of a slightly informal FAQ, even for a stuffy corporate site. It's the one place you can really let your hair down and seem human, without it taking away from your site. Now, I'm not advocating saying, "Right on, dude ... "

on a million-dollar stock investing website (or anywhere, for that matter), but answering questions with an informal, "Absolutely!" or a, "You bet!" isn't going to hurt you, and may just tilt that one person a year in your favor.

Q: One person a year? What the heck does that mean?

A: The things that I am discussing in this book will all help you have a better website. I'm just trying to point out that it's these small details that make the biggest differences. Perhaps bolding a certain word gets you one client more a year. Perhaps making the story subheadings I discussed earlier gets you five more a year than if you didn't have them. Perhaps that slightly informal FAQ answer gets you one extra client. I know from experience that these things happen.

Remember something: Every reader is an individual person. They will contact you for different reasons. For example, I have a funny line involving a yak way down on my website writing page. I had a guy contact me saying that line made him laugh, and he thought my writing was exactly what he was looking for ("serious, but in a casual way" was how he put it). He turned out to be a $10,000 client. That one line probably tipped him into contacting me instead of another writer. A $10,000 line, that was. Another client mentioned my informal FAQ. Another mentioned how my services page spoke directly to him ... etc. All of these things contribute to a successful website.

Q: So inserting a small joke or the like is okay in an FAQ?

A: For the most part, small jokes are okay in FAQs. I'm not saying you have to be a comedian, but even for the most high-level sites, it's generally okay to be a little irreverent in an FAQ answer or two.

Personally, my FAQ is conversational, and mostly serious. Then I have this one question:

"Are there any subjects you won't write about?"

Not really. As long as what you want me to write is legal, I'll probably do it. I don't allow personal beliefs or agendas (if any) get in the way of my writing. However, I will draw the line at promoting what I see as hate or discrimination. This means I won't be writing the KKK's Christmas letter anytime soon.

Ha ha. A riot a minute, aren't I? Actually, in five years, this FAQ answer has been commented on several times (and always in a positive way). Did it tip the scale and get me an extra client or two? Maybe. I know it's not hurting me (well, the KKK will probably choose another writer, but that's fine).

Q: How long should an FAQ be?

A: Ten questions minimum. If you can't find ten things to talk about in an FAQ, you aren't trying very hard. And maximum? Well, as long as it needs to be. If it's long, you can use the "anchor link" thing I discussed earlier to get all the questions up top, and when someone clicks on them, they jump right to the answer. Just, if you do this, make sure you have the list of questions up top as anchor links, PLUS the Q&A within the body. Like this (I've shortened this and pasted it into Sample 19 so you can see what I mean. On my website, the link list is a LOT longer — you can't see the first question unless you scroll, which is okay).

Q: Any other FAQ facts I need to know?

A: No, I think that about covers it. Just make sure you have one. A lot of people (like me) almost always read the FAQ of any website they're even remotely interested in.

FAQ EXAMPLE

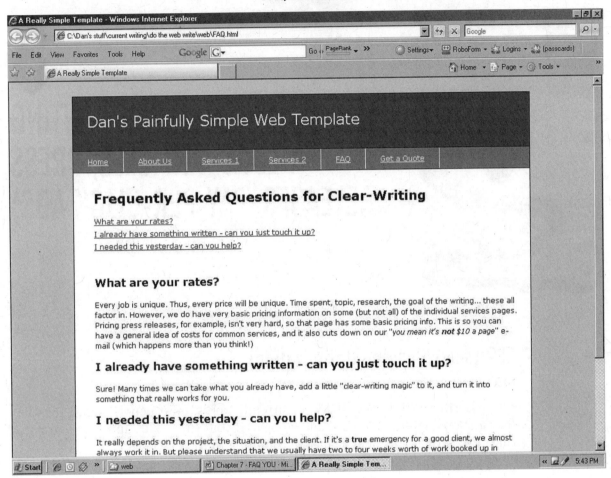

8

SEO AND "TRAFFIC"-TYPE WRITING (BLOGS, ARTICLES, PRESS RELEASES, PAY-PER-CLICK ADS)

SEO (Search Engine Optimization)

SEO (Search Engine Optimization). It's on everyone's mind.

And why not? The way the web currently works, most people search for what they are looking for on Yahoo! and Google. If your site comes up in the search results, you have an excellent chance of capturing traffic.

This chapter will be devoted to writing to get traffic. This means we'll discuss some SEO stuff, and to a lesser extent, pay-per-click (PPC) ads. We'll start with SEO.

SEO Explained

SEO stands for "Search Engine Optimization," and generally refers to the things you do to your website that will ensure it ranks near the top in results for particular search terms. In other words, if someone searches for "professional writer," I'd really like to be near the top of the search results.

The keyword myth

I already mentioned this once, but it is worth repeating: There is a big misconception that having keywords in your text is all you need to achieve a high ranking. I say this because I'm in the business of writing for websites, and let me tell you, a very high percentage of people I talk to seem to feel keywords = high ranking. That's simply not true.

Keywords are almost the last thing you need. Yes, they matter; the search engines will look at your site, and yes, they want to see keywords/keyphrases. But they want to see a TON of other stuff more.

Now, this isn't an SEO book, and I'm not an SEO expert, but from my experience and knowledge, here are a few things that are more important than keywords:

- ✏ **Inbound links from other sites (in particular, highly respected sites, and sites in your industry).** In other words, if people in YOUR industry think you are worthy, they will link to you. This can be tough, because your peers are often your competition — why would they link to you? (Quick note — if your business is limited by geography, like a plumber, it might be a great idea to exchange links with other far away plumbers.)

- ✏ **Your site structure.** The hidden back end of your site matters a lot. Page titles, headlines, link anchor text — this all matters (this is why I advocated using H2 subheadings, etc.).

- ✏ **Updates.** Search engines like content-rich sites. Having useful articles, and posting new ones frequently, is a great way to get both traffic and links. Having a blog helps too.

- ✏ **Other links.** Again, articles come into play here — writing articles for other sites, having press releases, etc. — these are all great traffic builders.

The preceding, at this writing, are all more important than simply putting keywords in your text (in my opinion). And much of it involves writing.

Now again, this isn't an SEO book — I can't tell you how to build your site for search engines (the search engines change the rules all the time anyway). But since we know articles, blogs, and press releases are important, I CAN help you there.

But before I do that, I want to talk some smack about SEO companies.

Beware of SEO companies

I want to go on record here and say that I am not a huge fan of SEO companies. To me, they could be considered almost fraudulent.

There are literally thousands of companies out there that are in the SEO and web traffic business. Most of them promise to get you high "natural" rankings on the search engines. In my experience, I've found perhaps 5% to be worthwhile, honest, up-front, and effective. The other 95% are crooks, plain and simple. So when you are dealing with SEO companies, here are a few things to watch out for:

1. **Stay away from any company that promises you a top ten (or top anything) ranking:** This is BS, and I'll illustrate that with a simple numbers game: what if they promise 11 similar companies a top-ten ranking for the best keyword? That simply doesn't work. Take my company, for instance — there are hundreds (and even thousands) of writers out there. We all can't be "top ten" for the keyphrase "professional writer" (or all the other good keywords), can we? So promising is out. A good SEO company will deliver measurable results without making extreme promises.

2. **Stay away from companies that get you good rankings for lousy keywords/ keyphrases:** This relates to point one … if they can't logically deliver the top keywords to everyone, many unscrupulous companies will instead seek to pacify the unwary by getting them top rankings for terrible keywords. Allow me to illustrate.

   Once a company hired me to help them with their website, and in our initial conversations, they said they were working with an SEO specialist that just delivered them a number one Google ranking, and boy, were they happy about it. The company in question sold fruit baskets. Now, the SEO specialist couldn't deliver a top ten ranking for "fruit baskets" or anything even remotely similar, because all the top positions were taken by well-established companies.

   Instead, this SEO specialist conned the fruit basket company into paying thousands of dollars to get a top ranking on "monthly surprise basket club" — that was the top-ranking keyphrase that everyone was so juiced over. Now, this kind of made sense to the fruit basket company because, well, they DID have something they called a "monthly surprise basket club" (obviously, the SEO company saw that and pounced, saying, "Hey, you want to push those monthly surprise baskets? Then let us get you a top ranking for them").

   But let's be honest, how many people do you think type that exact phrase into Google a day (and it had to be the exact phrase for it to come up first)? I'm going to guess pretty close to zero. I mean, do people really search for fruit baskets by typing in "monthly surprise basket club"? I would think not … I would think the word "fruit" would have to be in the search, right? But if the word "fruit" was in the search, this poor company was ranked about 200.

   I told the company my feelings, but they were not swayed. They LOVED the fact that they had a number one ranking on something.

   As it turned out, I was right (big surprise there). Two months went by, and not one person — not one — came to the website through that phrase. In other words, having a number one ranking for that phrase was completely useless. They may as well have had a number one ranking on "Godzilla delivers eight pizzas daily" for all the good it did them. (Please note: To protect the anonymity of my client, I have changed the search term and the industry in the preceding).

So if you are going to have a specialist handle your SEO, make sure it's for good keywords and keyphrases. Otherwise, a great ranking is completely useless.

3. **Stay away from companies that write like fourth graders:** I'm probably not being fair to fourth graders here (because my fourth-grade niece Erin writes better than these morons). Allow me to illustrate:

Once a slimy SEO company called me, and tried to persuade me to use them by showing me other websites that they got top rankings for. One of them led off with these words (no lie):

"Buy New York Car Tires in NY from a New York Car Tire Company that specializes in automobile tires in New York. Car Tires in New York and automobile tires in New York should be purchased from a NY Car Tire Company that services car tires in New York for Automobiles in New York. Car Tires for the lowest prices in NY for your New York car tire needs."

Um … do you think they sell car tires in New York? I copied that verbatim — a website REALLY did that.

I don't know how effective this is in terms of actually closing the sale, but I'm pretty sure I'd rather entrust my car to people who can write somewhat coherently. Something telling: The company that wrote that since changed their site to a more conventional site, because I'm sure the preceding gobbledygook resulted in poor sales.

Okay, now that I've ensured no SEO company will be sending me a Christmas card (along with the KKK), let's get to SEO writing.

SEO Writing

Besides the keyphrase stuff I previously went over, there are three other types of writing that will help in your SEO efforts: press releases, articles, and blogs. Let's take them one at a time.

Press releases

In terms of the Internet, press releases are generally news about your business that, if interesting enough, get picked up by news websites. The up-front use is to tell something newsworthy about your business. The hidden (and oftentimes real use) is to create more links to your site, get some advertising in, and produce yet another page that may come up in search engine results.

Internet press releases have exploded in popularity for a simple reason: As of now, they seem to help in generating decent traffic and SEO rankings. If the press release is interesting enough, it will get a healthy online distribution. Even if it's only marginally interesting, it will probably get at least a little play in your industry (because it's free content for many websites). Plus, often when a release of yours is posted somewhere, it hangs around for a long time.

Simple math dictates that the more press releases you release, the more you have out there. And if they stay online for awhile, it starts to build upon itself; if you do a release a month, you have 12 out there in a year's time, 24 in two years. And because all of the releases will link back to your site, that's a good thing.

For several years now, I have been writing press releases for several clients on an ongoing basis, and today when I search for those clients (or even search for what they do), a good chunk of the search results are to the press releases I wrote. That never hurts.

On the CD that accompanies this book, there's some good PR information: There's instructions for the structure of a press release (to help you write your own), there are two sample press releases, and there's a link to www.PRweb.com on the Internet Resources file (PRWeb is one of the places you go to "release" press releases).

I'll also briefly go over writing press releases here.

Writing press releases

Most important rules:

- Rule 2 (short paragraphs)
- Rule 6 (keep your audience in mind, etc)
- Rule 11 (be an Oreo — make your company something special)

Press releases seem complicated, but they aren't. Not at all.

The main thing to remember is that I am talking about online press releases, as opposed to traditional print and newspaper press releases. They are very different (not many traditional press release people will admit this).

Traditional print press releases were (in my opinion) 70% for public relations, and maybe 30% for marketing buzz. They had arcane rules, they had strict formats, they could only be "released" by insider "PR pros" ... in short, this wasn't something you wanted to take on yourself.

Online press releases are (in my opinion) 20% public relations, 30% marketing buzz, and 50% SEO. And with the vast size of the Internet and the "release them yourself" websites like PRWeb, this has meant a definite relaxing of what constitutes a true press release. These factors combine to make online press releases much easier to write.

So, for this book, I'm going to show you how to write and release online press releases to get you a little buzz, and give you some links.

All news, all the time (so they say)

The one thing traditional and online press releases have in common is the news aspect. Even online, a press release still needs to have news, and not be a preachy ad. For example, it cannot blatantly say, "So visit company XYZ because they have the lowest prices." It has to be written from an impartial, third-person angle. Essentially, when you write a release, pretend you are a reporter writing a story.

Getting around the "news" requirement

The first thing we need to remember is what exactly constitutes "news" is always subjective, but to make it easy for you, let's say it has to be the introduction of something new on your end. New building, new website, new page on your website, new offer, new delivery truck, new delivery route, new delivery charge, new office furniture, new policy, new way of doing things, new chair ("Tight Feet Shoes Has Remodeled"), new tree outside ("Tight Feet Shoes Goes Green!"). Even a new observation like, "Hey, we're now getting email business — we need a new computer" can be turned into a press release proclaiming, "Email Orders Mean Expansion for Tight Feet Shoes." In essence, anything new can generally be made news.

I use the "new" scenario because it's a very easy place to start. Certainly you can think of something new for your business, right? After you write a few and get comfortable, feel free to expand on the new. But start there, as it's easy to remember (and write).

Sneaking in some advertising

Press releases are not supposed to be ads. But it's pretty easy to sneak in plenty of advertising. Just quote yourself, someone in your company, a customer, etc. ("We started this business because nobody within 30 miles sold low-cost Cow Wash," said owner Gertrude "Gerti" Huffernagel. "So with some seed money and a lot of sweat, 'Bovine Buff' was born").

You can quote almost anyone — yourself, someone in the company, a customer, your mom — just make sure you have permission to attribute the quote to them. I do not advocate the simple making up of quotes and using names without permission.

In a nutshell, it's simple. Find a news angle (any news angle), write a little story on the news angle (go ahead and have some fun with this), and quote yourself (or someone in your company, a customer, etc.), to give the advertising angle.

As easy as 1,2,3

Okay, let's stop for a second, because I can hear it now: "But Dan, this advice somewhat makes a mockery of the traditional news requirement. This isn't what the pros say about press releases!"

Again, I am not teaching you a "traditional" press release. Most information you see about writing a press release assumes an old style release. I'm showing you how to write a press release for online purposes (generally, to generate some interest and SEO). In essence, you can say writing online press releases is as easy as 1, 2, 3.

1. Pick something new for your news angle to write about.

2. Write as a reporter, and also quote yourself or someone in your company a few times.

3. Have fun.

That's it — that's generally all there is to it.

Okay, okay, there are a few structural things (I go over these in a detailed "how to" on the CD included with this book, but I'll outline it here too). Your headline needs to be in title case (the first letter of the main words are capitalized) and have no punctuation, the second headline needs to expand on what the first headline said. And in the release itself, the first few paragraphs generally need to tell the who/what/where part of the story, and there's an about the company at the end.

That's pretty much it in terms of "rules." But it's better to show you than to tell you. Just follow my examples, and you'll be on your way.

On the CD, I have two actual press releases that I used for my first book (I decided that wherever possible, I wanted to use true-to-life examples — hence REAL press releases that I actually used), plus press release how-to instructions that will go over the entire structure of the release. In addition, here's one of the releases printed in Sample 20:

Let's look at this release for a second and go over structure:

- There's the contact information — I usually put my phone and email in too, but for this book, I'll leave those out.

- Then there's a headline in title case (meaning the main words are capitalized, and no punctuation is used).

- There's a second headline (not in title case) that expands on the first headline.

- The city and date.

- Then I get into the story — I start with an anecdote that I quote myself, and then get into the meat of the release (about the book, etc.).

PRESS RELEASE EXAMPLE

PRESS RELEASE

Contact Information:
Dan Furman, CEO
Night Owl e-Ventures Inc.
www.clear-writing.com
www.danfurmanonline.com

New Book Offers Help to REAL People Who Want to Start a REAL Home Based Business

Fed up with silly scams, useless information, and increasingly weird multi-level "opportunities"; entrepreneur / business author Dan Furman gives owners of REAL home based businesses the success formula they are looking for.

Kingston, NY. August 23, 2007. It was the packet of green jelly that finally struck home. Business copywriter and marketing consultant Dan Furman remembers the product well:

"A client was starting a new home based business, and wanted me to write copy for a new multi-level marketing product she would be selling – a "healthy" gel snack, sold in foil packets" said Furman. "Essentially, it was a packet of goo. I thought to myself 'this is just going too far. Why can't people just start REAL businesses?'"

Furman, an owner of a home-based copywriting and marketing business, decided to write a book detailing the ins and outs of running a real business in (or out of) your home. The book is entitled "Start and Run a Real Home Based Business", and is now available at bookstores nationwide and online retailers like Amazon.com as well.

The book details Furman's expertise on the subject of running a home based business, expertise gained from years of being in business himself, both in success and failure. It's also aimed at owners of what Furman calls "real" businesses.

"Nothing against wannabe mystery shoppers, scrapbook party-givers, or the latest multi-level fad, but in my mind, those aren't *real* businesses" says Furman "When you talk about a REAL home based business, you're talking about a web designer, a plumber, someone who runs a daycare out of their home, a pet sitting service, a contractor, a writer like me, someone who makes a product and sells it online, etc. That's who this book is for – people who want to start those businesses, or already own them and want some tips on running them."

Furman's book is broken up into 55 topics essential to home based business owners; each running anywhere from two to five pages each. The tone is also decidedly blunt, and rather funny as well "I want people to read the book and learn from it. What better way to do that than make someone laugh?" states Furman."My entrepreneurial career has been filled with all kinds of funny stories, and I'm not shy about telling them, even if some of the mistakes I made were a little embarrassing."

About Author/Entrepreneur Dan Furman

Dan Furman is a professional business writer, entrepreneur, and business author. His new book is entitled "Start and Run a Real Home Based Business", and is packed full of information that any home based business owner will find extremely useful. The book is also funny as heck. You can read about the book at its websites: www.startandrunarealhomebasedbusiness.com or www.danfurmanonline.com. Dan is also the owner of www.clear-writing.com, a professional business writing service.

- I then quote myself again for effect (to get in more marketing-speak), and then end it with a quick summary and yet another quote. I went heavy on the quotes here, but I think it works for this release.

- Lastly, I have the links in the contact information. I could have put a link in the main body too, but decided the one on the bottom was enough.

Essentially, this is a press release about my (at the time) new book. That's the news angle — a new book being released is definitely news. I write this from an outside perspective, and quote myself several times. I also try to be a little interesting / funny with the packet of goo (true story). This was a pretty successful release (even generated a few phone calls from news-type people and got me an interview or three. I also got a call from an infomercial guy about perhaps selling my "system," until I explained my book was actually "anti-system." Still, it's nice to get phone calls like that, and hey, you never do know where things like that will lead).

Again, there's nothing complicated here. Simply remember the basic structure (and almost all release websites — where you have to go to release them — will have basic instructions on structure), and follow the 1, 2, 3.

I recall doing some training with a company; I was there to teach the marketing department some of my writing concepts. I told them my "1, 2, 3" theory on press releases, and one person — her name was Nancy I believe — commented on how simple I made it sound. She was reading a book on press releases, and the book made it seem so complicated and arcane. She liked my way a lot better, and went on to write a bunch of really good releases.

Follow my simple instructions here, and you'll start writing better press releases almost right away (trust me, they are really fun to write. Anytime you can quote yourself it's fun).

Keywords and links in your press releases

Like any other online writing, get a few keywords and keyphrases in your press release. But again, like everywhere else, you need not force them, just be aware of them and use them where they logically fit. The same goes with links.

In fact, the same goes for articles and blogs as well (which we'll get into in a moment).

One and done? Not by a longshot.

A lot of people become disappointed when they release a press release. They expected to release one press release and have the world beat down their door and their website rise to the top. That's not the way it works.

See, the main goal of press releases (as they relate to SEO) isn't to necessarily get someone to read the one release and say, "Holy @#$%, I need to contact these guys!" It's instead meant to just give you little more ammo out there in your overall marketing efforts. And yes, each release adds another piece of ammo to your over-all efforts. They put you out there and they link back to your site. Don't be the company that does one release and then says the next day, "Well, THAT was un-derwhelming." Trust me, you will release your one press release, and likely will wake up the next day to a largely unchanged world in regards to business. Press releases are not one and done. You have to be consistent in writing and releasing them (actually, this is true with all of these SEO things I am talking about).

Okay, we're done here. Let's move on to articles.

Articles

Most important rules when writing articles:

- ✐ Rule 1 (keep it scan-able — headlines and subheads are important for articles)
- ✐ Rule 2 (short paragraphs)
- ✐ Rule 7 (write with confidence)

Writing articles is actually pretty easy and fun. That's because there really aren't any rules regarding structure, form, or content. Almost anything can be called an article.

The main things to remember in article writing are the goals. The goals are twofold:

1. You want the article to paint you as an authority. Articles are a great way to proclaim, "I am an expert in my industry." Even if your articles are just on your own website, they definitely help in boosting your status.

2. You want the article to get put on other websites. You do this by offering use-ful information — make the article useful enough so someone else would say, "This person knows his or her stuff." This helps get your article placed on other websites.

How to write an article

So knowing our two goals, let's go about writing an article. To make things easy, I am going to give you the lowdown on two fairly simple types of articles. I'm doing this because it makes article writing far less intimidating for those who have not done it before. Almost anyone, of any writing skill level, can write an interesting article if they choose one of the following two types.

The "list" article

The list article takes your expertise and breaks it down into a list. For example, if you are an accountant, you can make a list article entitled "Seven Hidden Tax Deductions You Need to Know." If you are a plumber, it can become "Five Signs Your Hot Water Heater is on the Fritz." And the list points can be short (a sentence or two even). This makes list articles a very easy entryway into article writing.

The list article is also a good way to break Rule 5 and preach to the choir. For example, I could (and probably should) write an article entitled "Ten Reasons Why You Need a Copywriter." (I'll get right on that after I finish this book.)

All you need for a list article is a quick opening paragraph introducing the list, and then get right into the list. You can then have a quick sentence (with your website link) to wrap it up. On the CD, I've included a (fairly sarcastic) list article entitled "How to Make Your Website Fail." Just reading it should give you the basic form and structure regarding list articles (not that you will need such — I'm betting you can write a basic list article right now).

I like list articles because they are simple. Anyone, and I mean anyone, has the knowledge to write one. Even someone in jail could write a list article entitled "How to Stay Out of Jail."

Which brings me to another point: The "how-to" makes a great list article. Either a list of separate points (like my CD sample) or a numbered step-by-step list, a "how-to" makes for a very interesting and valid list article.

Again, the list-type article is very simple, and I fully recommend that you start there. In fact, you can start and STAY there, too. I have seen many businesses successfully use articles in their marketing, and never go beyond writing list-type articles. But if you want to branch out, here's a place you can go next …

The story article

The story article is something you should try after you do a few list articles and get the posted in a few places. The story article is exactly what it says it is; it's an article that tells a story.

Now I recommend you try this one second, because it is definitely harder. I feel anyone, of any writing ability, can write a list article. Especially after reading this book (it should be a no-brainer, in fact). But the story article, well … there's no way I can teach you to tell a story. You either can, or you can't. So why am I including this?

I'm including it because there are a ton of you out there who have a little writing talent, and you don't even know it. You may not have written anything since high school (and we all know how I feel about how they do things), so I'd like to challenge you to write a story article once you feel comfortable with articles. Trust me, I'm not going to grade your paper. I won't even see it. But I want you to write a story article on the following subject: How did you arrive at your current position?

Really: Write an article that explores how you got to where you currently are. You can make it funny, make it "lite," include a few bullets or subheadings if you wish. There are no rules (except for my rules … well, you don't need to write your story with a lot of "yous" so you can ignore that one). But really, just let it flow.

The importance of my picking that subject should not be overlooked. Every article (list, story, etc.), begins with the subject. Pick something you know a lot about (and I expect that you know a bit about yourself) and just start writing from the heart. And don't be afraid to have a little fun — remember, nobody is grading this.

On the CD, I've included a story article about the importance of having a nice home office. As you'll see, I veer off wildly into other areas. I think it's pretty obvious that I had fun with this one. In addition, I also include a "hybrid" type article (written by a friend) that combines a story beginning with a list.

Now, if you write a story article and you hate it, that's fine. You tried (which is what I really want you to at least do: try it). It's okay; not everyone will write an interesting story, no matter how many rules I teach you. If that happens to you, write list articles instead (or start a small story then veer off into a list). As I previously mentioned, many, many people do just that, and that's perfectly okay.

How long should an article be?

An article should be as long as it needs to be, really.

A good minimum is, say, 250 words (which isn't a lot at all). I find my average length is about 350–500 words (let that be your sweet spot). But I've gone higher (my story article on the CD comes in at almost 800). Just remember, the longer you go, the more audience you will lose (but the audience you keep probably likes you more with each word, so this angle has its pros and cons).

Can your articles be funny / creative?

If you wish, yes, your articles can be funny and creative. To be honest, almost all of my articles have a bit of humor / irreverence in them (it's just how I write). So yes, you can get witty and creative if you want to. However, you do not NEED to be. A serious "Ten Tax Strategies for Mayonnaise Manufacturers" is just fine (well, that might be hard to write about without a giggle or two … apologies to Hellmann's).

What do you do with articles once you write them?

To begin, start an articles page on your website — post the articles (or at least links to them) there. This helps with the "your site is consistently updated" part of SEO (which is vital — in general terms, search engines give more weight to websites that are frequently updated.

In addition to (or instead of) that, post them to message forums you frequent. Submit them to article submission sites (search Google for these). Start a MySpace or Facebook page and post them there. Get them on DIGG (again, search for information on this ... the new buzz-term to look for is "social media marketing," or "social networking marketing." Essentially, these terms refer to social media websites like MySpace, Facebook, and the like).

You can even offer them as a free download from your website. People love free information.

Or you can post them to your blog ...

Blogs

Blogs became this big buzzword a year or so ago; it seemed everyone said you had to have a blog on your website. And they are right — it IS good to have a blog on your website. They help with SEO, they help with client retention, they help sell "you." They are very useful.

What to write in a blog

To begin, articles are great blog posts — and I already went over articles, so there's no need to revisit them. But I will say they don't all have to be full articles. They can just be mini thoughts on topics that pertain to your business. Like Sample 21, which I wrote on June 21, 2007. Not even 125 words. And it's a valid, useful blog post.

But they don't always have to be useful. A blog can be very informal and chatty at times. I always found it useful to mix hard-hitting articles with jokes, simple "how-to" thoughts, quick "just crossed my mind" posts, and the like. I even sneak in a post about fantasy football (a hobby of mine), an occasional movie review, or maybe some vacation pictures.

To give you an example of a "non-useful" post, Sample 22 is something I posted the day before the preceding "write out numbers" post.

Now, the point I'm making here is to be HUMAN. I've seen way too many blogs that are nothing but on-topic articles and soft "It's Halloween — time to clean out your business cobwebs"-type posts (groan). It's like they are afraid to post something that isn't about business. That's silly.

You know what? Instead of the soft "we're being cool by recognizing Halloween, but it's still a business post," there's nothing wrong with posting a trick-or-treat story on Halloween, or maybe some pictures of your staff in costume. Or tell me about the fire in the cafeteria ...

What I'm trying to say is, mix up your posts. Make a good three quarters of them useful on-topic business articles (both normal articles and short "quick thought" posts), but make the other 25% fun — something that interests you, your staff, etc. Trust me — I have learned this from experience — the more human your blog is, the more people will come back and read it.

SAMPLE 21
QUICK BLOG POST EXAMPLE

<u>**A quick writing thought**</u>   *Posted On 2007-06-19, 8:06 PM*

Someone asked me about this today, so I thought I'd pass it on:

When you are writing numbers, generally one thru ten are spelled out. The rest aren't. So we spell "seven", but not 17.

I break this rule often, though (it's not really a rule, but more of a handshake agreement.) Why do I break it? Because "we handle any size job, from 3 pages to 300" catches the eye better than "we handle any size job, from three pages to 300" (although the second one actually looks more professional when reading - so it's really about what you are after - scan-ability, or a professional read.)

Anyway, just thought I'd share that.

Keep your blog current

Many businesses fail to keep their blogs current.

Once started, you have to keep your blog current. That means two to four posts a month at a minimum (some blogs seem to post everyday/every other day, but I don't know too many people who can keep that up). Even once a week is a lot for many businesses.

To me, two to four posts a month is a nice sweet spot for most product/service-type businesses. But if you can't commit to two to four posts a month, don't start the blog. It will hurt more than it helps.

That's because NOT keeping your blog current says one thing: "We start things we don't finish." This is a terrible message to send. Don't be like that.

Two to four a month. It's just not that hard.

NONBUSINESS / HUMOROUS BLOG POST EXAMPLE

<u>**Spam Subject Lines**</u> *Posted On 2007-06-18 6:37 PM*

Spam e-mail subject lines are funny. I don't trust spamblockers, so I get it all. Here are a few that I recently got (my comments in the smaller, italic text):

Big Your Piano - Be a Real Man *(what??)*

Emanuel Sando has been plagued by a series of spills at big-time events!! *(who?)*

New way to give her pleasure that she always dreamt!

Jackhammer Millie!! *(I'm assuming this is the pleasure Millie dreamt of?)*

Museum Hysterectomy!

Give little bro another few inches *(err... no)*

Cordela sent you a zebowel.hk greeting *(yea, choose "zebowel" as your domain name - that'll get me to click.)*

Biggerer *(I assume this was conceived by the same person who came up with "it's thickerer" for the 1970's era "Chunky" candy bar commercials.)*

She waits for you by cold river *(Millie, I hope)*

Some final thoughts on SEO

Before I move on into discussing pay-per-click ads, I want to give some final thoughts on SEO. Here we learned about the "outside" writing that helps with SEO (blogs, press releases, and articles), and we also went over why I hate most SEO companies and why I think keywords are somewhat overrated by many. But I want to sneak in a final thought or three regarding SEO.

I feel this entire SEO business of trying to trick out the search engines is silly. I have a theory on good SEO, and from my experience, it seems to work (I'm in the top 20 of many of my best keywords). Here it is:

Just be the best website you can be.

Really, that's it. Be the best site you can be. Have solid information on your website that someone looking for your product/service will find useful. Branch out and help people by writing articles. Participate on forums with your website link in your signature. Consistently post to your blog. Update your website every so often with useful information. Keep the world abreast of what's going on by releasing a press release every so often.

Do these things, and be a little patient (as it takes awhile), but your site will definitely rise in the rankings.

Be the best site you can be, and your ranking will eventually take care of itself. And if you feel you need an expert's help, find a good SEO company (one that doesn't make outlandish promises; good ones DO exist) to help put you over the top.

Okay, let's move on to pay-per-click ads.

Pay-per-click (PPC) Ads

Pay-per-click (PPC) ads are a boon to many, and the object of scorn for others. But they can make your online business very successful, so it's important to go over them here (at least in a writing sense).

A very quick primer

When you search for something on a search engine, two sets of results come up: the "natural" or "organic" rankings, and sponsored ads (usually on the top and the right hand side). Those ads are pay-per-click ads. They come up when people search for the terms you choose, and they see your ad. You pay when someone clicks on your ad.

PPC ads will cost you money. There is no way around that fact. For just about any industry, all the decent keywords cannot be had for the minimum bids.

But let's not get into ad budgets here. You want tips on writing your PPC ads, and I'm here to help (if you need to learn more about the technical aspects, the search engines have all the information you will need).

Writing PPC ads

You can go to Google and learn everything about PPC in terms of how to set up your ads, what keywords to bid on, how much to bid, etc. But they don't offer you too much in writing them. So let me help by offering you several key points (I'm doing it this way as it's easier to digest. You need not do ALL of these in every ad. Actually, given the space limitations, you won't be able to. These are just food for thought when writing PPC ads).

- ✎ Address the reason they searched. Again, like I mentioned way back, people are searching for you for a REASON. If your ad addresses that reason, all the better. One of my ads says that I offer "Crisp, succinct business writing that gets you results." Most people who searched for me are looking for business writing that gets them results, and here I am offering it (change out "web copy," "website writing," "letters," etc., for "business writing," for the same result on different keywords).

- Tout a benefit. The "that gets you results" part of the preceding example is a definite benefit.

- Include your keywords in the ad copy. This might mean setting up different ads for different keywords, but that's okay. For example, for the keyword "business writing," I have "business writing" in the ad. This grabs attention, and for some search engines, the search terms are bolded (nice!) It might also be a crucial tiebreaker in who gets their ad higher.

- Get the word YOU in there if you can. And I did just that in my preceding example.

- Use your town/city/state in some ads. Even if you serve the world. It addresses those people that still search for something local.

- Test headlines. Sometimes, you may want the headline to address the reason they searched (e.g., "Professional Writing"). But other times, you may want to test different catchy ones (e.g., "Need Top Notch Writing?") Either are valid. TEST, my friend, TEST.

- Use symbols if you can. Some PPC search engines allow the equal sign (=) for example. This looks interesting in an ad: "Our writing = more profits for you".

- Ask them to click (or don't). Some people may think a "click to find out more" will work. It may, depending on your ad (again, test these things). But remember, you may only get 30–35 characters a line, and two to three lines to tell your story. They already know to click, so perhaps telling them to do so isn't the best use of the limited amount of characters you get.

- Prices generally don't belong. Again, you can test this, but every time I have put prices in my ad, I have been disappointed with the results.

- Make your ads work WITH your website. If you say you have a deluxe widget in your ad, the deluxe widget should be the first thing they see on the page the ad goes to (in other words, make sure your landing pages correspond. If you click on an ad for X, you don't want to land on a page that shows Y).

That last point is my lead-in to the next chapter. Your PPC ad does NOT have to go to your home page, or even to your main website. Since you control the keywords that trigger the PPC ad, and you also control the page that the ad points to, you control the content that the person sees.

Read on …

9
ALTERNATE LANDING PAGES AND MICROSITES

One of the most powerful techniques available in regards to websites and website conversion is the alternate landing page and/or microsite. It's also what I like to call an "oh yeah … " marketing tool, because when I talk with many companies, the very thought of having another website (or alternate landing page) never occurred to them. Yet, once you think about it, it's almost obvious that it's a good move. It also works extremely well with pay-per-click (PPC) advertising.

The Concept Behind Alternate Landing Pages and Microsites

Essentially, the idea behind alternate landing pages and microsites is this: Since a website is most effective when it speaks to targeted traffic, doesn't it make sense to make your website (or landing page) itself as targeted as possible? Yes, it makes a lot of sense.

But that brings us to a problem: A company website has one home page, and the company does a lot of things. How can you make that one home page speak to a particular audience? For example, let's take my website. I'm a writer. I write web copy, I write letters, I write proposals, etc. My home page speaks to all of these audiences.

But, as we've learned in this book, the better that you directly address your visitor and solve their problem, the better you will convert. Hence, the more targeted you can make things, the better off you are. So knowing that, isn't it to my advantage if I can somehow just talk about letters to the people who came for letters, and just talk about web copy to the people who came for web copy?

Of course it is. So how do I do that?

Simple. I make a PPC ad that targets the keywords for letter writing, and I point that ad not to my home page, but to my letter writing services page. Then, I make certain my letter writing services page is written like a home page (which isn't that much different anyway).

The result is profound. The people who click on my letter writing ad get taken directly to my letter writing page (which is exactly what they are looking for). So doing things this way, I directly address the reason these people are coming.

This can be taken to almost any extreme. Let's say a plumber offers water heater installation as a service. He or she can have a water heater installation PPC ad, and have that page go directly to the water heater installation page. And their general plumbing ad goes to the home page.

Do you see how powerful that can be? The water heater prospects don't have to click around the home page and guess if their problem will be solved; they clicked on a water heaters installation ad, and get taken not to a general plumbing page, but right to a water heater installation page. This makes converting prospects that much easier. And of course, if the product / service is big enough, you can give it its own separate microsite, instead of a separate landing page.

Okay, that's the basics. Let's look a little closer at alternate landing pages and microsites.

Alternate Landing Pages

These are exactly what they sound like; you set up an inside page of your website (almost always a Service or Products page) as BOTH a normal services page and a landing page. In reality, this is very simple to do. All you need to do is write the copy in a similar style to your home page. Simply assume this page is the first page a visitor sees, and that visitor is expecting that particular product / service.

Okay, so what are the differences in the page? Well, re-read Chapters 3, 5, and 6 if you need to, but in a nutshell, a landing page is a little more scan-able, and doesn't preach to the choir as much. It also somewhat welcomes the visitor, and lets them know you can handle their issue/need right away.

In other words, a quick writing adjustment is usually all that's necessary. For me, when I made my letter writing page a landing page, I simply made it a bit more scanable, and changed the opening text. In other words, I made my letter writing page the home page for those seeking letter writing (even though technically, clicking

"Home" in my navigation bar took them to the real home page. Trust me, nobody notices, and it makes no difference. You need not fret over your page names, etc.)

There's a screenshot in Sample 23.

Notice that I even went as far as to add a quote form RIGHT ON THE PAGE.

What this does is it allows the prospect seeking a letter to get a quote right away; no messing around with other pages. You need a letter? Boom — get a quote for your letter right here, right now.

I can't begin to tell you how much better this works than having my letter writing prospects go to my home page.

Alternate Landing Pages and PPC Ads

While you can use alternate landing pages without PPC, they do work exceptionally well with PPC ads. With PPC ads, you can capture web surfers on a keyword-search basis, and then deliver them to the page that directly addresses their needs (what they searched for). All you need to do is set up different ads (and thus, different target pages) for different keywords (your PPC provider will tell you how to set up different ads).

Now, you don't need to do this for every service you offer. Myself, I do letter writing and website copy. I could choose to also do this for my other services like press releases, etc., but I choose not to spread myself out that wide (no real reason except that I just don't want to solely push press releases).

Alternate landing pages are a great way to boost conversions. If you have a specific service that people search for, this is one thing you definitely should explore. As a plus, once they are made/changed, alternate landing pages are essentially free (no new hosting, etc).

This brings us to microsites.

Microsites

Microsites share the same concept as alternate landing pages, except they do it on a larger scale. A microsite is essentially a small, stand-alone website (generally three to five pages, but can be as small as one page) that usually focuses on a single product, service, or theme.

Microsites will have their own domain name (that you buy), and may or may not be on the same hosting account as your main website (more on hosting and names at the end of this chapter).

ALTERNATE LANDING PAGE EXAMPLE

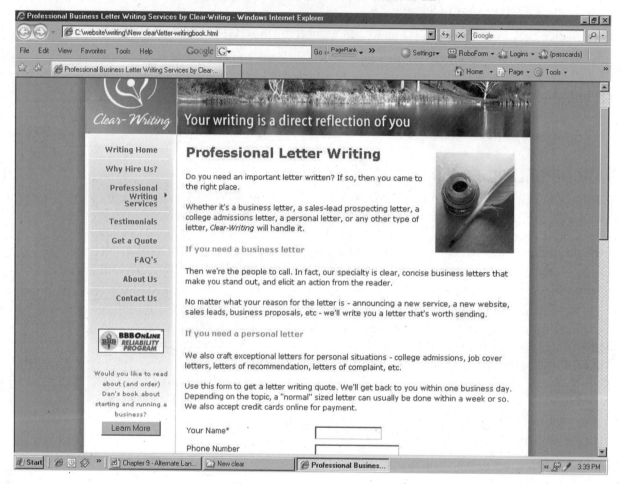

To give you a better example of what a microsite is, instead of my one letter writing page, I could have small letter writing website (www.clear-letters.com or something like that. I actually bought that domain in case I decide to do this).

The advantage here is that I would have an entire website devoted to letter writing. I can do a five-page home, why us, letter writing services, get a letter writing quote, and FAQ targeted just at letters. This is even more powerful than the alternate landing page, and is usually the next step to take (which I'll probably take once I get a few spare hours)!

You can do the same thing with the PPC ads. They will point to the new microsite instead of your main site.

This allows you to really expand and sell a particular product or service. Three to five pages (it can be any number really, but I find this to be the sweet spot) gives you ample room to discuss features, benefits, why to use you, etc. This makes converting visitors easier. There are a few other advantages, too.

Other advantages of using microsites

- They give you another "real" website out there, increasing your overall presence in your industry.

- You can link your main site to the microsite (and vice-versa), helping each with SEO.

- Testing is a little easier with two sites: You can test something on one, while the other churns along unchanged (helpful if the test bombs).

- The microsite can be so tightly focused that it truly makes you an expert in the particular specialty.

- The cost is nominal — domain names are shockingly cheap, as is hosting. Plus, a three to five page site need not be complicated at all. At this writing, I can have a microsite up and running for less than $200 (that's for the entire year).

I made a microsite for my last book, and will make another one for this one (it will be at www.dothewebwrite.com). A microsite lends an air of credibility and professionalism that an alternate landing page just cannot. And for the price, it becomes a no-brainer.

Now, having a microsite does not mean you won't offer the same service/product on your main website. Indeed, your main website still might get you the bulk of your business for the particular service. But the microsite allows the tight focus that perhaps the main site cannot give. I highly recommend trying one.

Domain names and hosting for microsites

For a microsite, you'll always buy a new name (why wouldn't you?) But there's the question of hosting … you can buy a new hosting plan for it (like you have for your main site), or you can have it on your main hosting account, and have the name forwarded to it (because technically, the URL would be www.yourmainsite.com/micrositepagenames.html. Forwarding masks this somewhat).

Now, some may argue with me, but I am not a fan of shared hosting/forwarding. I think you should just buy a new hosting account for your microsites.

To begin, if the websites share a host account, if the one server goes down, you totally go dark (i.e., you have no live web presence). Spreading out your websites over different hosting companies is sometimes the smarter move.

Also, I think it hurts you with SEO. Having two sites on the same server linking to each other is almost certainly not seen in the same light as two totally different websites linking to each other. Now some people online will argue this they say there is no difference. Others say there is. But, just from a pure logic and reasoning standpoint, the more I think about it, the more I have to agree that it would hurt you in SEO. I don't care about virtual hosts, masking, etc. (don't mean to get all techie on you). I'm not entrusting my business / SEO / etc. to the opinion of message forum blowhards (which is what the people arguing this stuff are).

I look at it this way: If my microsite can't justify the (almost always less than) $200 a year that hosting would cost, it's simply not worth having. I'm not going to mess around with this. If I have a good enough idea to have a microsite, it's worth my buying a hosting account for it. Just something I've learned over the years — don't be cheap when it comes to business.

That said, there's nothing wrong with placing it on your current hosting account and forwarding TO TEST IT. In the beginning, yeah, go ahead and do the forwarding thing. But as soon as you know it's viable, get a hosting account. That's my advice anyway.

Now, I want to clarify something. In my opinion, it's FINE to have several domain names pointing to a site (I do this myself). THAT aspect of forwarding is fine (as I'll show you in a second). One site with ten domain names pointing to it is fine. It's when ten different sites share one server; that's what I think is bad.

Bottom line: In my opinion, I think each hosting account should host one site only.

A Quick Thought on Domain Names

I buy a lot of domain names. Most I don't use (nor will I ever use them). So why do I buy them?

Well, the answer is simple: Sometimes I get the inspiration to perhaps make another microsite, offer another service, or branch out my business into another industry. If I find an available domain that fits, I buy it right then and there for a year or two. Total cost is perhaps twenty bucks. And if my idea ever evolves past the "maybe I should do this" stage (most don't), I'm ready to go with an excellent domain name.

For example, I loved this book title — I had the domain name secured before I had the book idea sold / contract signed. I figured I'd use the name to make an informational site or something, but then as this book took shape, I realized it was perfect for the title. By the way, I bought www.dothewebwrite.com AND www.dothewebbright.com (because if I tell someone the name over the phone or such, they will almost certainly spell it "right"). I'll simply point the "right" one to the "write" one (this is a case where forwarding is useful).

I recommend buying domain names whenever you get an inspiring idea. They're cheap enough, and you never know. Perhaps it helps you see a good idea through to fruition. You need not buy them for a long time to start (a year or two should suffice). And you need not do the whole .net / .org / .info thing either. And, of course, you don't need hosting until you actually decide to do something with it (and like I mentioned earlier, you can test on your current hosting account and use forwarding, although I do recommend moving it to its own hosting account if it's successful. Okay, enough with the technical stuff).

Well, that's it on alternate landing pages and microsites and such they can be an exceptionally powerful piece of marketing. They are also fairly obvious, but you'd be surprised at the amount of people who say, "Wow, I never thought of doing that" when I mention it to them.

Oh my goodness. I just realized that I'm almost at the end of this book. One more chapter of (more or less) random thoughts on websites, and we're all done. I hope you've found this worthwhile so far, and perhaps picked up a nugget or two (or ten) to use on your own website. Geez … I'm a little sad (I felt this way at the end of the last book too — obviously, I like doing this quite a bit).

Okay, I wiped my tear (not really, but it sounds neat). Let's move on to the last chapter.

10
DAN'S BONUS CHAPTER
(EVEN MORE FOR YOUR MONEY)

Okay, here we are at the end. I really did write this book in order, because in general terms, one part helps build the next. But in looking over my notes, there are a few things that just didn't fit into any other areas (or they were things that I wanted to reiterate), so I'll go over them here.

Why All of This Website Conversion Stuff Matters

To some people/companies, just "having" a website is enough. Those companies are destined to fail online. Think of your website as a store/office — in this day and age, you can't get away with a substandard store or office. Would you go take your car to get fixed at a shoddy looking garage with no signage and where you had to almost crawl under a car to find the mechanic ("Scooter 'Bust-a-Knuckle' Grimes at your service!") Or would you go to a clean shop with a reception person and plenty of information on services offered, etc? Unless you are deranged (or Scooter's relative … same thing), you're going to use the nicer shop.

It's the same thing online. You have to tailor your website to the wants and needs of your visitors (they want information, they need it presented in a clear, easy-to-work-with fashion). That's what I have been trying to teach you in this entire book — following what I laid out will result in a website that has the wants and needs of your visitor in mind. Which is the most important thing you can do.

Remember, your website is NOT for you —it's for your visitors.

I know I mentioned the preceding point earlier, but it's worth repeating.

Do Not Put Up Roadblocks

Get rid of the introduction flash movie. Lose the "log in before going any further" screen. These things do nothing but lose you business. I can't be any more succinct than that.

Stop Hiding Your Phone Number

Make it simple for me to call you. I mean, really, what is the point of not having your phone number on your company website? It basically says one of two things: "You are not important enough to talk to," or it says, "We can't afford to have someone answer the phone." Neither inspires confidence. Unless you are a huge, well-established company like Best Buy, Amazon, etc., I'm not going to do business with you if you hide your company phone number. I don't necessarily mean YOU PERSONALLY need to answer it, but people should be able to call your company.

Stop Scolding Me About Copyright When I Right Click

Some companies are so paranoid that someone is going to steal their images that they have an "anti-right-click" script that yells at me if I right click. Well, I'm an old techie, and right click does a lot more than "save pictures as." In other words, I use the right click a lot. Besides, you aren't stopping anyone. I can just swipe your pictures from my cache anyway (and if you yell at me, I might do just that out of spite).

If You Aren't in a Band, Don't Play Music

Most people do not like music that automatically plays when they visit a website. Maybe it's okay for a band, but that's about it. And I guess that would depend on the band, as well (meaning Midnight Death Screechers can forgo the music, too).

Keep Dates Updated

If you are going to have a blog, don't let it slide. If you are going to have company news on the front page, make sure it's current. Having news/dates that are over six months old is a turnoff. And having last year (or even older) … yikes. That tells me you don't keep stuff up. Old dates are the online equivalent of cobwebs.

Answer Your Email / Quote Form

This may surprise you, but I would say the overall response rate from most website contact attempts runs around 60% (this is based on personal experience). This means a full 40% of my requests for more information, customer service, etc., go unanswered. This is somewhat surprising, and fully unacceptable. Every email you get that is expecting an answer deserves one. Period.

Turn Off Your Spamblockers

Maybe the reason so many emails go unanswered is people are SO afraid of spam that they ask a program to sort their email and DESTROY ALL SPAM before it even gets to their mailbox. Unfortunately, it also destroyed my message because I used the phrase "increase the size of" in it ... Never mind that the full sentence was "I'm hoping your services, which I am planning to pay a LOT for, will increase the size of my business." Nope, the spamblocker saw "increase the size of" and figured I was peddling little blue pills (honestly, that's just a guess — I have no idea if they are really blue). So I got dumped (which, ironically, is something the little blue pill is supposed to prevent ...)

Spamblockers are silly, and are a detriment to your business. Get rid of them and start using your "delete" key on spam.

Make Sure I Can Do Business with You From Anywhere

Another quasi-repeat. For service websites, you should have a Quote page that's on the navigation bar (that's a given). But you should also have links from within the copy for when the navigation bar scrolls off the screen. Essentially, what I am saying is that no matter where I am on your website — no matter what part of the page is showing on my screen — I should see some type of link to get in touch with you.

Re-Read Chapter 4, Rule 7

I can't begin to tell you how much of a difference writing with confidence has made in my life.

Join and Participate in Online Forums for Your Industry

If you're a plumber, start reading and posting on plumbers/plumbing/home improvement communities and forums, etc. Find them by searching for them (and find the time for them by trading a little TV time for Internet time). Create a signature (almost all let you do this) that includes a link to your website, and start posting useful information (even just by answering the questions of others).

Write and Post Articles

Even if all you ever do with these is post them to your own website and/or blog, it will help build your credibility. Start with "how-to" list articles ("Top Ten Ways to Prevent Itchy Ears") and go from there.

Look At (and Learn From) Your Competition

Look at your competitors online, and learn something from them. If they are doing something you like on their sites, make it for yourself (don't plagiarize, however). But if your competitor has a neat quote form on the bottom of every page, and you like that, go ahead and have one for yourself made. And yes, this extends to other writers — if you see something on my website that you like, learn how it's done and create it for your site.

Be an Oreo (Again)

We already went over this in Rule 11, but find that special thing about yourself / your company and tout it. Remember: NOBODY CAN COMPETE WITH YOU AT BEING YOU. This isn't *Invasion of the Body Snatchers* — there's only one you (and only one company quite like yours). Use that uniqueness to your advantage.

Give Something Away

Articles offering free advice, printable downloads, etc., give something away. I have a page of free writing tips on my main website. It gives someone another reason to bookmark me.

Internet Success Comes in Small Increments

Despite the fact that overnight success is definitely possible online, the simple fact is this: Almost all successful websites got to where they are slowly. Overnight success is not what you should be looking for.

Success happens when you make some small changes to your website, and bump overall conversions by 1% (which, as we went over way back when, could really be huge increase in business). Then you make a few more small changes and get it up another 1%. Then you branch out and make an alternate landing page, and eventually, a microsite. Then you bump that site another 1% ...

It's all about making small changes, testing results, keeping what works, and building upon it.

Keep the Focus on Your Website Visitor

As you go through your website, constantly ask yourself, "What's in it for them?" Because, trust me, they are subconsciously asking, "What's in it for me?"

Check Under the Hood Often

Check your website often. Make sure there are no broken links. Make sure there is nothing that is outdated. Make sure your last blog post is still somewhat fresh.

Check your quote form — does it work?

I've included a short checklist called the "Check Under the Hood Website Checklist" for this on the CD.

Understand the Changing World

As I write this, the world is changing. I'm sitting here in my basement in upstate NY, wearing shorts and a NY Jets t-shirt. My wife says I need a haircut, and I last shaved two days ago. Most days, from all outward appearances, I am not the picture of "serious business." Yet, I do business with million-dollar companies all over the world (as far away as China, which is about as far as you can get from me).

Do you have any idea just how mind-boggling that is?

And I don't do this because I am some jet-setting go-getter. Literally, there are days when going to the mall (elapsed distance: 1.7 miles) is WAY too much for me. My website makes that all possible. This web thing is way beyond some fad — it's serious business, and you need to make it work for you.

Gas just passed $4 a gallon here. More and more economic rumblings mean more people will stay closer to home. They might shop more online. They might start working from home more. Maybe instead of going on vacation, they get something on their house fixed that helps save energy ... etc. Some people think these things are bad. I think they are opportunity for those that recognize such. I don't care what business you are in — there's opportunity for you in any economy. All it takes is an idea, a niche, and a microsite (you were probably waiting for me to tie this paragraph in).

Here's another change — I got yet another phone book/Yellow Pages the other day, and I threw it away. I literally don't own the Yellow Pages anymore. Google is how I find everything.

My point is this: The world is changing, and the power of the Internet is simply unrivaled in terms of business. It is simply the greatest marketing tool ever invented. Only the shortsighted can't see that — if your website isn't working for you, trust me, you are doing something wrong. Either in content, in marketing it, in the target market you are trying to reach ... etc. Find out what is wrong and fix it. Use this book to help.

I hope I've helped you in making your website work. I can't force you to incorporate anything I wrote here, but trust me here: I know — without question — that the things I talked about, and the tips I gave WORK. I live it every single day.

Okay, we're done. Best of luck to you in all of your business endeavors. And you'll be hearing from me again — count on it.

Dan

OTHER TITLES OF INTEREST FROM
SELF-COUNSEL PRESS!

Ask for these titles at your local bookstore
or visit our website at www.self-counsel.com

The Entrepreneurial Itch
David Trahair, CA
ISBN: 978-1-55180-735-5
$13.95 US / $17.95 CDN

Statistics say about two out of three small businesses fail within the first three years. Those are some very tough odds. And yet, every year, unsuspecting entrepreneurs show up at their banks asking for small-business loans. The problem is that far too many people go into business without doing thorough research into what it really takes to be successful. And the best way to do this is to learn from someone who has worked with hundreds of small businesses, just like David Trahair, who wrote this book to share his knowledge with you.

Writing Romance
Vanessa Grant
ISBN: 978-1-55180-739-3
$19.95 US / $24.95 CDN

Romance novels represent one of the most lucrative genres in book publishing — making up over half of all mass market fiction sold in North America and generating more than $1.2 billion a year. This book will show you everything you need to know to successfully break into the romance writing market, from planning and plotting your story to editing and selling your manuscript.

Whether you're excited by classic love stories or steamy erotic romances, there's a market for your love story. Let Vanessa Grant coach you in the process of getting from idea to finished novel.

Start & Run a Real Home-Based Business

Dan Furman
ISBN: 978-1-55180-866-6
$20.95 US / $23.95 CDN

If you're looking for yet another useless, "fluff-filled" book on home based businesses, then this book isn't for you. Instead, this book is for real people who want to run a real business, and the updated second edition contains even more tips for entrepreneurs.

Learn how to:

- Make good money working from home

- Profit from skills you already have

- Stop dreaming — start doing

Whether you want to work at home on your computer, open a daycare, start a local service (like a plumber, computer consultant, pet sitter, etc.), or anything else, then *Start & Run a Real Home-Based Business* is what you've been waiting for.

Writing Science Fiction and Fantasy

Crawford Kilian
ISBN: 978-1-55180-785-0
$16.95 US / $21.95 CDN

Are you struggling to get started on your science fiction or fantasy novel? Stuck at Chapter 2 or need a fresh approach? Find new direction and inspiration with this unique guide to creating original and convincing stories. Written by a successful author of more than ten science fiction and fantasy novels, *Writing Science Fiction and Fantasy* takes an in-depth look at these two best-selling genres. Learn how to:

- Develop believable fantasy worlds

- Challenge your readers' imaginations

- Master the craft of magical worlds